An Analysis of Differential Delayed Mortality Experienced by Stream-type Chinook Salmon of the Snake River:

A response by State, Tribal, and USFWS technical staff to the 'D' analyses and discussion in the Anadromous Fish Appendix to the U.S. Army Corps of Engineers' Lower Snake River Juvenile Salmonid Migration Feasibility Study

Nick Bouwes and Howard Schaller, ODFW
Phaedra Budy, USFWS
Charles Petrosky and Russ Kiefer, IDFG
Paul Wilson, CBFWA
Olaf Langness, WDFW
Earl Weber, CRITFC
Eric Tinus, ODFW

October 4, 1999

EXECUTIVE SUMMARY

In the Anadromous Fish Appendix of the US Army Corp of Engineers (USACE) Environmental Impact Statement on the Lower Snake River Hydrosystem Alternatives for recovery of Snake River salmon and steelhead (hereafter referred to as "A-Fish"), the National Marine Fisheries Service (NMFS) suggested that transportation effectiveness of spring/summer chinook may have improved markedly in recent years. The NMFS conclusion was based on estimates of 'D'-values (the differential delayed survival rate between transported fish and fish that migrated in-river) for 1994-1995 (NMFS, 1999). NMFS suggested, if 'D' is high (estimated in A-Fish at 0.8) **and** extra mortality of in-river and transported smolts is unrelated to the hydropower system, transportation options may meet recovery standards as well or better than natural river options. NMFS also suggested that further studies could reduce the uncertainty about true values of 'D' and provide greater confidence to make a decision on the alternative management action needed to recover listed Snake River salmon and steelhead. In this analysis, we demonstrate that the evidence is compatible with a wide range of 'D' values, but only a small portion of this distribution is as high as the A-Fish estimate. We also present evidence that the extra mortality of in-river fish is related to the hydrosystem.

We analyzed a suite of plausible assumptions used in the calculation of 'D'. Based on our analysis of the 1994-1996 PIT-tag data, there is a wide range of possible 'D'-values. The NMFS' estimate falls at the upper end of this distribution ($90^{th} - 95^{th}$ percentiles). Alternative 'D'-values, based on what we believe to be more reasonable assumptions, were closer to 0.48. Because 'D' is a modeled value (and not a measurement, as implied in the A-Fish), it is very sensitive to the suite of assumptions made and how the data are grouped. 'D' estimates were most sensitive to: (1) whether or not fish that were transported from downstream collection/transport sites (Lower Monumental (LMO) and McNary (MCN) dams) were included in the group of fish used to estimate transport smolt to adult return rates (SAR); and (2) how reach survival rate estimates were extrapolated down to Bonneville Dam (BON). In 1994 the 'D'-value estimated using four collection projects was much lower than two collection projects. However, in 1995 and 1996 the difference in 'D' using two and four collection projects was not as dramatic as in 1994. Therefore, the estimated high 'D'-values are mainly driven by this single assumption for one year. Based on past and proposed future transportation operations, it is unclear why fish transported at the lower two projects were excluded from the NMFS analysis.

Transported fish are subjected to stress, injury, and crowding at the collection projects. In addition, the physiological state of fish may be poorly synchronized with the time of saltwater

1

entry for transported fish. These factors could explain the higher delayed mortality experienced by transported fish as suggested by a consistently estimated 'D' value that is less than 1.

We disagree with the NMFS assertion that "ongoing direct experiments that contrast the return rates of tagged fish that pass through the hydrosystem versus the return rates of transported fish can resolve this question in a clear and unambiguous manner". While a few components of the 'D'-value estimate are measurable, the sensitivity analysis highlights differences in assumptions and uncertainties that are not likely resolvable in the near term. In addition, low numbers of returning adults and small numbers of smolts for wild spring/summer chinook salmon may hamper reducing the uncertainty in estimates for reach survival rates and SARs for a non-detected group. Therefore, data are unlikely to perfect our understanding of 'D' or eliminate the uncertainty in the most influential assumptions.

The hypothesis of extra or delayed mortality due to hydrosystem passage has an empirical basis, as well as biological rationale. Based on recent PIT tag data we also found evidence that delayed mortality of both in-river and transported smolts was related to hydropower. More specifically, the evidence suggests that, at least for collected and bypassed smolts, there is a difference between the patterns of direct passage survival rates and SARs. Smolts first detected and transported from the downstream projects (LMO and MCN) had lower SARs than smolts collected and transported from higher up in the system. Similarly (as reported in the A-Fish), SARs of in-river smolts decreased as the number of times the fish were collected and bypassed increased. These pieces of information provide evidence that the Snake River spring summer chinook extra mortality is related to the juvenile migration hydrosystem experience.

Based on results from life-cycle modeling (Marmorek and Peters 1998b), transport based management options lead to a high likelihood of recovery only when 'D' is high and the source of extra mortality is not related to the experience during hydrosystem passage. However, when extra mortality is hydrosystem related (which our analysis supports), the natural river options are still the most likely management action to recover these stocks, even if 'D' is high (which our analysis does not support). Simply studying 'D', if that were possible, without determining the source of extra mortality, yields little additional insight into effects of the different management actions on Snake River spring/summer chinook recovery. Given the dangerously low level of these populations, we do not believe it is prudent to make management decision on the configuration and operation of the Snake and Columbia hydrosystem for the next 5-20 years (i.e. delaying a decision preserves status quo configuration), based solely on one optimistic assumption about the effectiveness of past and current hydrosystem operations.

INTRODUCTION

Mass transportation of juvenile fish in the lower Snake River was initiated in the late 1970's in an effort to reduce mortality of salmon and steelhead during downstream migration. Fish are transported in barges and trucks to below BON, thereby circumventing direct mortality due to passage through the hydroelectric projects and reservoirs. Measurement of the efficacy of smolt transportation has taken the form of studies of "T/C" (transport/control) ratios. These mark-recapture studies measured the smolt-to-adult return rates (SARs) of test fish, which were transported, and control fish which were returned to the river (Figure1). These studies estimated the relative effectiveness of transportation to improve survival rates of fish from the site where they were collected as juveniles back to (usually) the same site when they returned as adults. Included in this T/C ratio is any differential mortality from the collection point to the end of the hydrosystem (to BON tailrace), as well as any differential mortality from below BON to the adult recapture site(s).

Although fish generally appear to survive reasonably well while in the trucks and barges, it is harder to gauge how well transported fish survive below BON, after they are released and continue their life cycle in the estuary and ocean. From the T/C ratios derived from transport studies, and estimates of "control" survival rates (through the hydrosystem) and direct transport survival rates, the parameter 'D' can be estimated. 'D' is the differential survival rate of transported fish relative to fish that migrate in-river, as measured from BON tailrace to adult returning to Lower Granite Dam (LGR). A 'D' equal to one indicates that there is no difference in survival rate (after hydrosystem passage), while a 'D' less than one indicates that transported fish die at a higher rate after release, than fish that have migrated through the hydrosystem. Results from the life-cycle modeling assessment indicate that recovery success of a particular hydrosystem management option for Snake River spring and summer chinook salmon is strongly influenced by the 'D' value (Marmorek et al. 1998). One reason 'D' is influential is that hydrosystem management options either rely on a transportation based approach (A1 and A2) or an approach that returns Snake River and Snake River/John Day portions of the hydrosystem to a natural river (A3 and B1, respectively). The value of 'D' has recently become a major focus of evaluation of recovery efforts for Snake River salmon and steelhead.

NMFS suggests there may be partial support for delaying a decision to breach the lower Snake River hydroelectric dams because 'D' estimates, using *"improved methods provided by PIT-tag technology"*, appears to be high for the recent past (A-Fish). Based on these estimates, NMFS further suggest that *"ongoing experiments by NMFS are likely to resolve the uncertainty regarding differential delayed transportation mortality in 5 to 10 years."* Alternatively, the Plan for Analyzing and Testing Hypotheses (PATH) analyses include a larger set of T/C studies and stock recruitment data that suggests 'D' is low, which lends support to breaching of the four

Snake River dams as the most robust hydro action for recovery of Snake River salmon and steelhead (Marmorek et al. 1998).

In addition to differential delayed mortality of transported fish relative to fish that migrate in-river, estimates of extra mortality have been made (Marmorek and Peters, 1998 a and b). Extra mortality is defined as any mortality occurring outside of the juvenile migration corridor that is not accounted for by productivity parameters in spawner-recruit relationships, differential survival rate of transported and non-transported fish ('D'); or common year effects (Figure 1). Thus, extra mortality is the remaining mortality after accounting for all other sources of mortality. Three general hypotheses have been proposed to explain extra mortality: the hydrosystem, reduced stock viability, and/or an ocean regime shift (Marmorek and Peters, 1998 a and b).

In this paper, we evaluate the NMFS conclusion that 'D' is now much higher than previously thought (A-Fish), demonstrate the sensitivity of estimates of 'D' to the numerous assumptions required to make an estimate of 'D', clarify and discuss the evidence for and against various interpretations of these assumptions, and discuss the possibility of improving estimates of 'D' in the future. We note that 'D' is not a measurement. Instead, it is an indirect estimate from data and requires numerous assumptions, with many different possible interpretations. In our analysis we evaluate the effect of these different assumptions on 'D' estimates: 1) including and excluding different control and transport groups; 2) using different techniques to expand reach survival rate estimates from a shorter experimental reach to the entire migration corridor; 3) using different approaches to weight cohort reach survival rate estimates to produce seasonal estimates; 4) using different approaches to summarize experimental groups on a daily or on a weekly basis for wild fish only or wild and hatchery fish combined; and finally 5) using different approaches of pooling or averaging estimates across years. In addition, the effects of using alternative tools (passage models) to estimate reach survival rates on 'D' value estimates were evaluated.

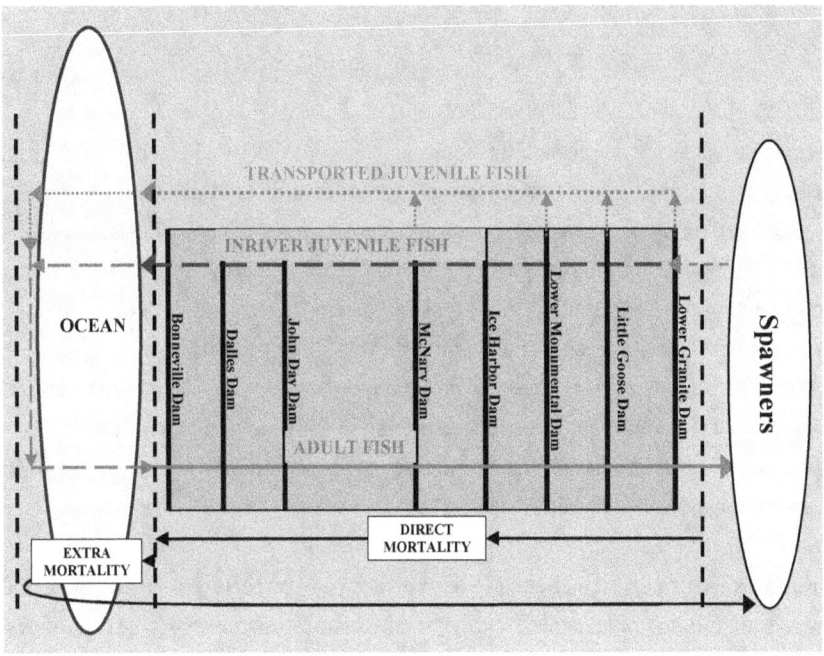

Figure 1. Schematic diagram showing the Snake River salmon and steelhead migration through the hydrosystem, from above LGR to below BON, through the ocean, to return as spawners.

METHODS

'D' is the ratio of post-BON survival rate of transported fish to in-river fish. In order to estimate 'D', survival rate of transported fish and fish that migrated in-river would have to be measured after fish passed BON. Measures of the number of PIT-tagged smolts passing LGR that return as adults (smolt-to-adult return rates) have been observed for transported (SAR_T) and for in-river (SAR_C) fish. This measurement includes survival rates through the hydropower system for transported (V_T) and for in-river (V_C) fish. Therefore, to estimate post-BON survival rates this hydrosystem survival rate is removed from the SAR values. 'D' is thus calculated by dividing the SAR_T/SAR_C by V_T/V_C where:

$$D = SAR_T/SAR_C * V_C/V_T$$

For example, if transported fish have a survival rate of 98% until release downstream from BON (value assumed in the NMFS A-Fish and PATH) and in-river fish have a survival rate of 33% downstream of BON (nearly 1/3 that of transported fish), and if transported fish return at a survival rate nearly 3 times that of in-river fish (SAR_T/SAR_C or the 'T/C ratio') then this would suggest delayed mortality were equal between transported and in-river fish ('D'=1). If transported fish returned at a survival rate of only 1.5 times that of in-river fish, then this would suggest delayed mortality of transported fish was double that of in-river fish ('D'=0.5).

The estimate of 'D' is accomplished through a series of computational steps, which rely on a number of assumptions. In this analysis we explored the effects of different assumptions on 'D'-values. We have summarized the computational steps into seven categories and have described and provided rationale for alternative assumptions in each category. We then calculated 'D' for most permutations of these assumptions across all categories to produce a distribution of 'D'-values. We use this distribution as the context for the 'D'-value NMFS has produced in the A-Fish. We also calculate an alternative 'D' based on the assumptions we believed are most representative of the conditions experienced by fish in the time period in question. We use both the NMFS set of assumptions and the alternative set of assumptions to explore the influence each assumption has on the calculation of 'D'.

The categories we examined include: the time period (94-95, or 94-96); aggregation method of the time period (pooled or geometric mean); methods of estimating V_C (passage models or CJS models with different expansions, weightings, and groupings); number of transport projects used to estimate SAR_T (2, 3 or 4 projects); detection histories of smolts to estimate SAR_C (non-detected, or non-detected and bypassed at MCN only, or non-detected and bypassed at MCN only, LGR only, and MCN and LGR); where fish were release to determine SAR_T, and SAR_C (above LGR or above and at LGR); and the determination of arrival numbers at LGR (methods developed by NMFS or by IDFG; Table 1). As stated above, the calculation of 'D' requires choosing a V_T value. The survival rate of smolts from point of collection on barges or trucks and release downstream from BON has never been formally estimated. In all estimates of 'D' by Marmorek et al. (1998), the NMFS A-Fish, and in this analysis, an assumption of constant $V_T = 0.98$ has been made. This assumption may introduce substantial error if actual V_T varies with hydrological and ecological factors encountered prior to collection, or if differences in handling during collection and release from barges or trucks influence survival rate.

Time Period

The NMFS estimate of 'D' was based on information for migration year (MY) 1994-1995. During these years PIT tag studies provided information that could be used to estimate some of the components of 'D'. This information has also been collected for subsequent years. Prior to 1994, PIT tag studies were not available to make estimates of 'D'. For the earlier years, the estimates relied on freeze brand and coded-wire tag studies for reach survivals and T/Cs.

Table 1. Categories and assumptions used in the 'D' sensitivity analysis.

Year	Aggregation	Vc			Transport groups	Detection History	Release Site	LGR arrivals
		Expansion	Weights	Groups				
94-95[a]	pooled[a]	CJS			LGR, LGS[a]	nd 94 nd, LGR, MCN, LGR+MCN 95,96 [a]	above LGR [a,b]	NMFS [a,b]
94-96[b]	geometric mean[b]	by project[a]	1/RV [a]	all fish daily[a]	LGR, LGS, LMN	nd 94 nd, MCN 95,96 [b]	above and at LGR[a]	IDFG
		by mile[b]	1/RV * PI [b]	wild fish weekly[b]	LGR, LGS, LMN, MCN [b]			
		Passage models						
		model CRiSP FLUSH	turb T4 T5			nd = non-detected		

[a] represents the assumption NMFS used to estimate 'D' in the A-Fish report
[b] represents the assumptions used in an alternative estimate of 'D'

Aggregation method for years

While 'D' estimates are calculated for individual years, like NMFS, we emphasized using multiple year estimates to characterize 'D'. Therefore, individual years need to be aggregated to provide an overall estimate of 'D'. In the A-Fish, NMFS pooled smolts and adult returns for MY 1994 and 1995 to get an estimate of 'D'. The potential problem with this method is that more weight will be given to years with the largest sample sizes. Therefore, this bias is simply an artifact of the sampling design employed for a given year and not a reflection of the 'D' for a given migration year. We believe a more appropriate approach to aggregate multiple year 'D' estimates is to use the geometric mean of the yearly 'D'-values.

Vc **method**

There are no direct measures of annual survival rate of in-river fish (V_C) that exactly match the reaches around which smolts are transported. The annual V_C's were estimated through expansion of reach survival rate estimates calculated from Cormack-Jolly-Seber (CJS) recapture models, or from passage models. Because we are estimating an annual 'D' value, the assumptions we explored that may have potentially affected the annual V_C calculated from the CJS model included: the cohorts of release fish studied; the weighting procedure used to calculate a seasonal survival rate estimate; and the expansion method used to extrapolate beyond study reaches.

CJS reach survival rate estimates

PIT tag information was collected from PITAGIS and compiled into a database by Fish Passage Center. The program MARK Version 1 (White, 1999) was used to estimate reach survival rates. As we produced nearly identical reach survival rate estimates as Smith (1999) for daily release of hatchery and wild fish combined, we defer to the NMFS estimates for consistency in comparing NMFS 'D' analyses in A-Fish with these analyses.

Study groups. Reach survival rate estimates used to calculate V_C by NMFS were based on daily releases of both hatchery and wild fish (all fish; Smith, 1999). Because 'D'-values and the SAR values used to calculate 'D' are specific to wild fish, reach survival rate estimates based on wild fish only may be more relevant to these analyses. Due to small sample sizes, estimates of reach survival rates for wild PIT tagged fish are often not possible on a daily time step. In fact, daily cohorts of all fish often have to be combined to get a reach survival rate estimate (Smith 1999). These small sample sizes on a daily time step also result in large confidence intervals around survival rate estimates. To avoid the problem of small sample sizes, we used weekly cohorts. An average annual survival rate is used to estimate 'D', therefore we believe seasonal differences in survival rate estimates are captured at the weekly time step. Because we produced nearly identical reach survival rate estimates as Smith (1999) for daily, all fish combined groups, we defer to the NMFS estimates for consistency in contrasting NMFS' reach survival rate estimates using daily cohorts of all fish with those using weekly cohorts of only wild fish.

Weighting cohort survival rates . To calculate annual reach survival rate estimates from the daily or weekly PIT tag data groups, each individual cohort survival rate estimate should be weighted to determine the appropriate contribution to the aggregate estimate. We used two methods: method 1 used in NMFS' estimates of 'D' weighted only by the inverse relative variance (Smith, 1999); and method 2 (which is more consistent with the way annual reach survival rate estimates were calculated for passage model calibration and validation used in PATH, Marmorek et al., 1998a) weighted by the inverse relative variance (1/RV) and normalized passage index (PI).

Weighting the individual cohort survival rate estimates by the inverse relative variance (method 1) results in greater influence for those cohorts with more precise survival rate estimates, and removes the influence of the survival rate estimates themselves (Smith 1999). Weighting these estimates by a measure of precision (inverse relative variance), but also by a measure of the portion of migrating population represented by the timing of each PIT-tagged group's migration past LGR (method 2), accounts for the fact that cohort survival rate estimates are not constant over the season, and that those study cohorts that coincide with greater portions of the population at large should make greater contributions to the annual survival rate estimate. The passage indices (PI) for wild yearling chinook, provided by Fish Passage Center (Portland, OR) were used to represent the population at large. The number of smolts, as measured by the PI for that day (week), was divided by the total number of smolts for the season, to estimate the contribution of that daily (weekly) cohort to apply to the survival rate estimates. In the work presented here, method 1 was used for the all fish daily PIT tag data and method 2 was used only for the wild, weekly PIT tag data.

Reach survival rate expansions. With either of the methods described above, it is necessary to adjust the study reach survival rate estimate to match the control reach (i.e., LGR tailrace to BON tailrace) in order to estimate V_C and 'D'. We employed two alternative methods: method 1 (used by NMFS) expanded the study reach to the control reach by calculating a per-project survival rate, and raising this rate to the power of the projects (control reach number of projects/study reach number of projects); and method 2 calculated a per-mile survival rate for the study reach, and expanded it to the control reach, by raising the per-mile rate to the power of the miles (miles in control reach / miles in study reach). Using method 1 implies the assumption that survival rate is the same for each project, despite great variation in project length, predator concentrations, temperatures, etc. Using method 2 implies the assumption that mortality from passage through reservoirs and dams is related to the length of reservoir the fish must traverse. We contrasted the method of extrapolating survival rate by the average per-project survival rate with extrapolating survival rate by the average per-mile survival rate.

Passage models

An alternative method of estimating V_C is to use predicted values from passage models. An advantage of using mechanistic or empirically-based passage models is that the assumption of constant survival rate per- project or per mile is not required to obtain estimates for reaches upstream or downstream from study reaches. Instead of relying on simple expansion of existing reach survival rates, passage models can predict survival rate over the whole system based on different hypotheses about the behavior of smolts and impacts of varying environmental conditions. In order to perform life-cycle assessments, it is also necessary to use some sort of model to predict in-river survival rate and other passage measures in past years without reach survival rate studies, and in all future years. We used estimates of in-river survival rates from both CRiSP and FLUSH. With FLUSH we used estimates made under different assumptions about greater (T4) or lesser (T5) historical dam mortality (CRiSP in-river survival rates are not influenced by differences in this assumption in years after 1980).

Release Site

In the A-Fish appendix, NMFS used fish released upstream from LGR in their 1994-1995 pooled estimate of 'D'. This release site most represents the impacts of the Lower Snake and Columbia River hydrosystem on SAR_C. NMFS calculated another 'D'-value for 1995 alone that included release sites upstream from and at LGR. The rationale for using this approach was that the influence of differences in LGR reservoir survival rate was negligible on overall SAR_C. We investigated the influence of the release sites upstream from LGR, and at and upstream from LGR on 'D' for migration years 1995 and 1996.

Transport Detection groups

Another major computational step in the 'D'-value estimate is determining the ratio SAR_T/SAR_C from LGR dam.

SAR_T = (transported adult returns at LGR)/(transported juveniles in LGR equivalents)

The estimate for SAR_T is affected by the collector projects selected. NMFS calculated SAR_T based on the smolts transported at only LGR and Little Goose Dam (LGO). However, in 1994-1996, fish were also transported at LMO and MCN projects. Including all collector projects accurately portrays actual transportation operations without biasing the overall SAR_T, because smolts and adult numbers from all collector projects are pooled when calculating a yearly SAR_T, and therefore, collector-specific SAR_T's are appropriately weighted. We contrasted estimates of 'D' using LGR and LGO only versus LGR, LGS and LMO versus all four collector projects.

The value of SAR_T is affected by the reach survival rate estimates because the smolt numbers collected and transported from the lower projects (LGO, LMN, and MCN) need to be converted into LGR transport equivalent smolt numbers (Sanford and Smith 1999). Whichever method was used to calculate V_C was also used to convert the number of smolts collected and transported from the lower projects (LGO, LMN, and MCN) into LGR transport equivalent smolt numbers.

In-river detection groups

For the in-river group,

SAR_C = (in-river adult returns at LGR) /(in-river juveniles in LGR equivalents)

is affected by the route of passage of juvenile fish. Snake River PIT tagged chinook that migrate in-river may pass through the bypass systems at transport collector projects. In contrast, all unmarked fish that migrate in-river pass the collector projects either through turbines or over spill gates. This is because PIT tagged fish are passed through the bypass systems, but all of the unmarked fish are collected for transportation. The route of passage can be determined by the detection history for PIT tagged in-river juvenile fish (e.g., fish never detected as juveniles, only detected at LGR, detected at LGR and LMN, etc.). NMFS evaluated specific detection history (by year) that varies depending on operations for a year.

The detection histories that NMFS used in 1994 included only non-detected fish. In 1994, fish that were detected at bypass/collector projects were transported. PIT tagged in-river fish that were collected at detection projects were returned to the river only for study. Therefore, the best representation of the population that migrated through the hydrosystem would be fish that were never detected.

The detection histories used by NMFS for 1995 include nondetected, LGR bypassed only, MCN bypassed only, and MCN and LGR bypassed fish. In 1995 and in 1996, fish were generally bypassed at MCN (not transported) and were diverted back to the river. Thus, in these years, fish released at LGR are best characterized by LGR only and LGR-MCN detections. However, fish released above LGR are best represented by nondetected and bypass only at MCN histories.

It appears fish released upstream from LGR were used in the 1994 and 1995 pooled estimate made by NMFS. However, in 1995 the inriver fish were still represented by LGR only and LGR–MCN detections. We chose to represent these fish released upstream from LGR with the detection history 'no detect' and 'MCN bypass only', as this best represents the experience of the inriver migrating population in 1995.

Fish that migrate in-river and have been detected one or more times have been shown to have a lower SAR, providing evidence for hydrosystem related delayed mortality (Sandford and Smith, 1999). Therefore, including multiple bypass fish may represent a lower SAR_C. A higher and more representative SAR_C, which would be expected under a maximized transportation management action (A2), would be based on non-detected fish only. In this analysis we contrasted multiple bypass detection histories with zero and single detection bypass histories in estimating 'D'.

As with the number of LGR equivalent smolts transported, the estimate for the non-detected juvenile numbers at LGR and those destined to be bypassed only at LGR are affected by the reach survival rate estimates method. CJS and passage model survival rate estimates were used to convert the number of smolts never detected into LGR equivalent smolt numbers.

Arrival numbers at LGR

The sensitivity analyses primarily used NMFS estimates for arrival numbers, with the IDFG estimates used for selected runs. The NMFS method (Sandford and Smith 1999) for estimating LGR arrivals summed daily passage estimates, which were calculated by dividing the passage index by daily detection efficiencies. The NMFS method defined a population known to be alive at LGR (by virtue of having been detected at LGO), and then determined the proportion of fish in the sub-population that was detected at LGR. Corrections were made for proportions of detected fish removed (transportation or unknown disposition) using 7-day running averages. The IDFG method (Kiefer et al., 1999) for estimating LGR arrivals was a one mark, multiple recapture method. This method used smolts detected and known to be bypassed at LGR as a mark group, smolt detections at the downstream collector dams as three separate capture groups, and subsequent detections of LGR bypassed fish as the recapture observations. To correct for different spill conditions at LGR, collection efficiency was regressed against spill proportion for the cohort.

Model Description

NMFS' methods for estimating 'D'-values were contained in a spreadsheet (Dcalc9496.xls), which was distributed in June 1999 to PATH members by Steve Smith, NMFS. However, the distributed model did not have the flexibility to do all the desired sensitivity analyses (e.g., different methods for reach survival rate or LGR arrival numbers), so we utilized one developed by Russ Kiefer and Paul Bunn (IDFG) for the primary sensitivity analysis. The two models used different data extractions (from PITAGIS, PSMFC database) for numbers of PIT tags in each detection history. The IDFG model was designed to allow the user to select different groups of in-river and transported smolts, different LGR arrival estimates, different reach survival rate estimates, and different methods of extrapolating survival rate to below BON. Smolt numbers, below-BON smolt numbers, adult numbers, and 'D'-value estimates are outputs. We compared 'D'-value estimates from the NMFS model and the IDFG model for a selected set of alternative assumptions and methods to determine whether the two models (and associated data sets) gave similar results.

IDFG developed a database that tracks the detection and disposition (bypass, transport, or unknown) of smolts at the collector dams, LGR, LGO, LMO, and MCN. Numbers of adults (excluding jacks) that returned to LGR from each of the detection history categories were determined from PITAGIS for each smolt migration year 1994-1996. Numbers of smolts in each of the detection history categories (including non-detected) were estimated in LGR-equivalents (Kiefer et al. 1999, Sandford and Smith 1999).

LGR-equivalents for first detections downstream from LGR were calculated by expanding observed smolt numbers in each category by the estimated smolt survival rate between LGR and the detection site. The IDFG model allowed the incorporation of alternative values of reach survival rate and alternative estimates for numbers of PIT-tagged smolts arriving at LGR (Kiefer et al. 1999 and Sandford and Smith 1999). Arrival numbers are used to estimate number of smolts in the non-detected category by subtracting the detected smolts in LGR equivalents from the arrival numbers.

After estimating smolt numbers by category in LGR equivalents, the next step involved estimating LGR-equivalent smolts downstream from BON. Numbers of below-BON in-river smolts were obtained as the product of non-transported LGR-equivalent smolts and the estimated LGR to BON smolt survival rate, based on various methods of estimating reach survival rate, and extrapolating reach survival rate to below BON. Numbers of below-BON transported smolts were the product of transport LGR-equivalents and an assumed transport survival rate of 0.98.

'D' sensitivity analysis

A 'D'-value was calculated for 120 combinations of assumptions across all categories for 1994-1995 pooled, 1994-1996 pooled, 1994-1995 geometric mean, and 1994-1996 geometric mean for a total of 480 'D'-values (*see* Appendix A --). We identified an alternative estimate of 'D' based on the assumptions we believe most represent current operations based on the rationale described above. Since it was not clearly defined by NMFS what detection histories they used for at and above LGR released fish we provided two NMFS 'D' estimates. The assumptions for the first NMFS 'D' estimate were as follows: evaluated in 1994 and 1995; aggregated through a pooling method; a CJS reach survival rate for all fish using 1/RV weighted mean daily cohort yearly estimates and a per- project expansion; transport groups from LGR and LGO; in-river groups with a detection history of non-detected in 1994, and non-detected LGR bypassed only, MCN bypassed only, and LGR and MCN bypassed for 1995; a release site upstream from LGR (Table 1). The assumptions for the second NMFS 'D' estimate were the same with the exception that a release site was used for above and at LGR in 1995. The assumptions for an alternative method to calculate 'D' were as follows: evaluated in 1994, 1995, 1996; aggregated by the geometric mean; a CJS reach survival rate for wild fish using 1/RV*PI weighted mean weekly cohort yearly estimates using a per- mile expansion; transport groups from LGR, LGO, LMN, MCN; in-river groups with a detection history of non-detected in 1994, and non-detected and MCN bypassed only in 1995 and 1996; a release site above LGR (Table 1). All 'D'-values were combined to create a distribution of 'D'-values to provide a context for the 'D'-value estimated by NMFS' set of assumptions and the alternative set of assumptions.

We attempted to balance assumptions of each category so as to minimize a bias towards certain sets of assumptions. For example, in PATH we examined the influence of greater and lower historic hydrosystem impacts on 'D'-values (T4 and T5) using two passage models, CRiSP and FLUSH. CRiSP estimates of hydrosystem impacts on smolt survival rate are lower than FLUSH. However, unlike FLUSH, CRiSP produces the same V_C under T4 and T5 for 1994-1996. We therefore included all 'D' estimates using FLUSH T4 and T5 and a double set of all 'D' estimates from CRiSP T4. Also, because IDFG arrival numbers at LGR were similar to NMFS' estimates, we ran only a partial sensitivity to this category. The only two sets of 'D' estimates using the IDFG arrival numbers were based on the NMFS first 'D' set of assumptions, and the other based on the alternative set of assumptions.

The influence of individual assumptions was explored by changing only the assumption in question and fixing the remaining set of assumptions. The fixed set of assumptions included the assumptions used by NMFS and assumptions of the alternative method.

Table 2. Reach-specific juvenile spring chinook salmon survival rate estimates by migration year. Estimates are presented under different groupings, weighting of in-season temporal estimates, and reach measurements.

Weight	Expansion	Year	lgr-lgo	lgr-lmo	lgr-mcn	lgr-bon	lgo-bon	lmo-bon	mcn-bon
All fish daily:									
1/rel.var.	project	1994	0.830	0.699	0.555	0.335	0.414	0.479	0.555
1/rel.var.	project	1995	0.882	0.815	0.715	0.557	0.606	0.659	0.716
1/rel.var.	project	1996	0.926	0.859	0.649	0.469	0.522	0.582	0.649
1/rel.var.	mile	1994	0.830	0.699	0.530	0.274	0.325	0.370	0.517
1/rel.var.	mile	1995	0.882	0.815	0.715	0.427	0.478	0.521	0.648
1/rel.var.	mile	1996	0.926	0.859	0.649	0.414	0.465	0.508	0.638
Wild fish weekly:									
1/rel.var.*PI	project	1994	0.846	0.754	0.568	0.372	0.440	0.493	0.654
1/rel.var.*PI	project	1995	0.895	0.811	0.681	0.510	0.570	0.629	0.749
1/rel.var.*PI	project	1996	0.950	0.869	0.594	0.402	0.423	0.462	0.677
1/rel.var.*PI	mile	1994	0.846	0.754	0.550	0.296	0.350	0.392	0.537
1/rel.var.*PI	mile	1995	0.895	0.811	0.681	0.456	0.510	0.562	0.670
1/rel.var.*PI	mile	1996	0.950	0.869	0.594	0.346	0.364	0.398	0.582

Note: Rel. var. = relative variance
       PI = passage index

Evidence of Delayed Mortality

We investigated evidence of delayed mortality for in-river and transport groups from the NMFS 1994-1996 data set. The data set was contained in a spreadsheet (Dcalc9496.xls) provided to PATH in June 1999. The NMFS estimates of SARs for transported smolts were examined for smolts transported from each of the four collector dams (LGR, LGO, LMO, MCN), 1994-1996. SARs for transport groups represented number of adult returns to LGR divided by the LGR equivalent number of smolts in each category. The NMFS estimates of SARs for in-river smolts were examined each year for groups that experienced collection/bypass 0, 1, 2, 3, and 4 times through the four collector dams. In-river SARs represented the number of adult returns to LGR divided by the LGR equivalent number of smolts in each category.

In addition to summarizing the observed SARs by route of passage, we estimated the expected direct dam passage survival rate for smolts in the five in-river categories (0, 1, 2, 3, and 4 collection/bypass experiences). Direct survival rates by passage histories through the four dams were calculated using PATH estimates of direct survival rate: 0.98, 0.90 and 0.98 for collection/bypass, turbine, and spill respectively. Reservoir survival rate was excluded from the calculations in order to evaluate only the route of passage. Expected direct dam passage survival rate ($ExpS_{byp}$) for the five passage histories was estimated as:

$$ExpS_{byp} = ([1\text{-}SPILLPROP][S_{turb}] + [SPILLPROP][S_{spill}])^{(4\text{-}byp)} * (S_{bypass})^{byp}$$

byp = number of times smolt was bypassed {0, 1, 2, 3, 4,}
SPILLPROP = proportion of non-bypassed fish spilled (assumed constant at 4 dams)
S_{turb} = Direct survival rate through turbine passage (0.90)
S_{spill} = Direct survival rate through spill passage (0.98)
S_{bypass} = Direct survival rate through collection/bypass system (0.98)

RESULTS

'D'-value estimates were very sensitive to combinations of model assumptions, methods, and definition of transport and in-river groups. Similar to the A-Fish sensitivity analysis, we report and emphasize multiple-year point estimates of 'D'. Confidence intervals around each point estimate are large (because of the small number of returning adults, variance around CJS estimates of survival rate, etc.); therefore, caution should be used in interpreting these absolute 'D'-values. Even when multiple-year point estimates were not sensitive to the different groupings or assumptions, individual year 'D'-value estimates were sometimes quite sensitive to these different groupings or assumptions.

In Figure 2, we present the distribution of 'D'-values estimated from the IDFG model (Kiefer et al., 1999), across 120 combinations of assumptions used to estimate 'D' for the categories of 94-95 pooled, 94-96 pooled, 94-95 geometric mean, and 94-96 geometric mean. This distribution of 'D'-values ranged from 0.02 to 1.07 with 'D' estimates at the 10th, 50th and 90th percentiles of 0.23, 0.52, and 0.78 respectively and a grand geometric mean of 0.48.

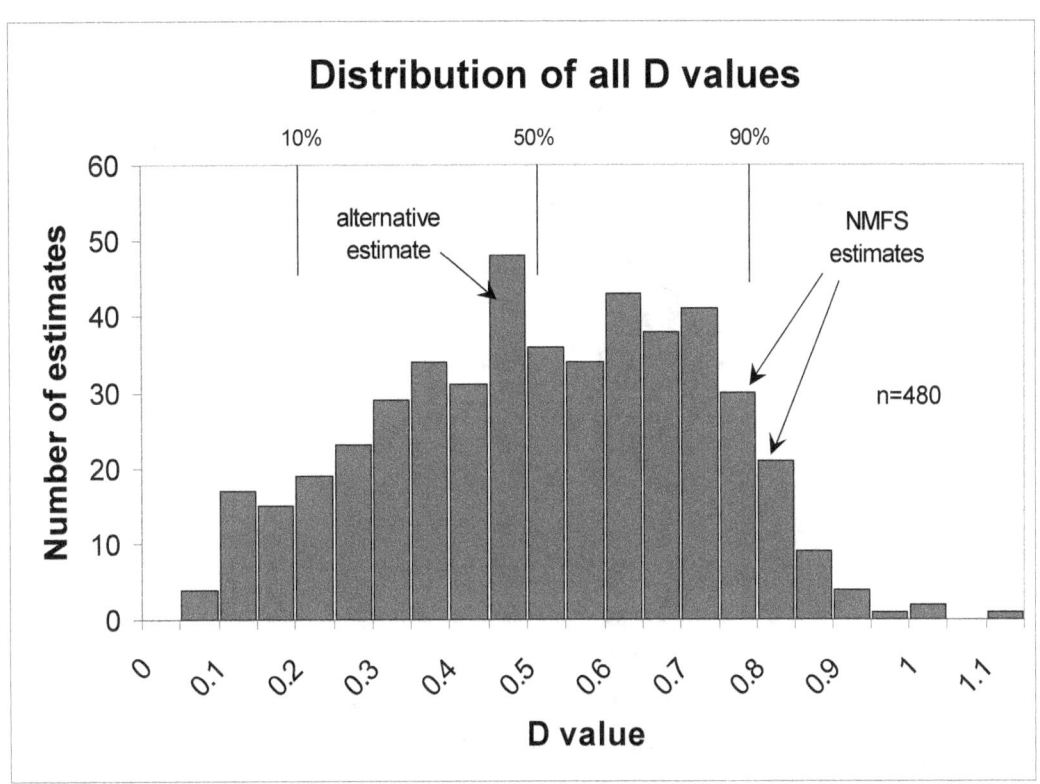

Figure 2. Distribution of 'D'-values estimates from the IDFG model across combinations of assumptions of all the components used to estimate 'D' for 94-95 pooled, 94-96 pooled, geometric mean of 94-95, and geometric mean of 94-96. Vertical lines represent the 10, 50, and 90th percentiles of the distribution. The values identified as the NMFS estimates were calculated with the IDFG model using the NMFS assumptions as outlined in the Smith and Williams response letter.

As described in the methods, we used the two sets of NMFS assumptions outlined in Smith and Williams (1999) and in the NMFS A-Fish in order to replicate the NMFS 'D' estimate for the 1994-95 pooled PIT tag information. Based on the NMFS assumptions, our analysis produced high 'D'-value estimates, which fell in the 89th and 93rd percentile of the distribution (Figure 2). We also compared the 'D'-values using the NMFS set of assumptions to the alternative set of assumptions. The NMFS first set of assumptions produced a 'D'-value of 0.77, and the alternative set of assumptions produced a 'D'-value of 0.48 (Figure 3).

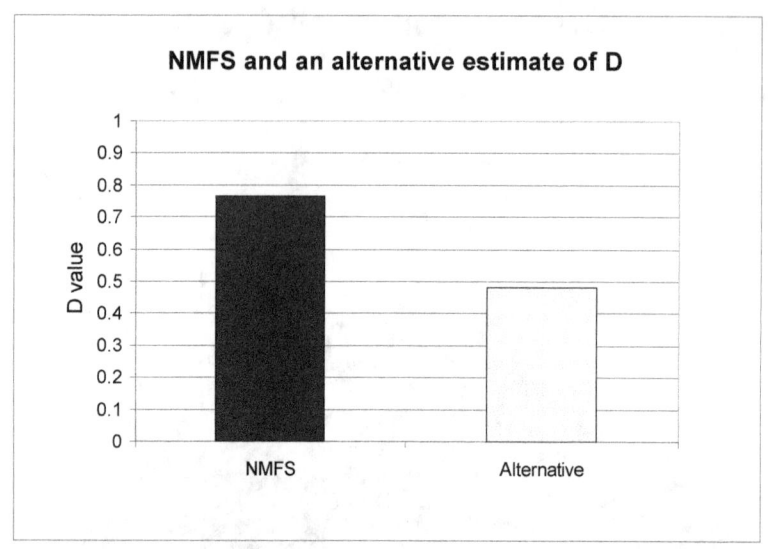

Figure 3: Comparison of 'D' estimates from models using NMFS' set of assumptions and an alternative set of assumptions for all components.

For this same comparison, the NMFS set of assumptions showed greater interannual variation in 'D' value estimates compared to the alternative approach (Figure 4).

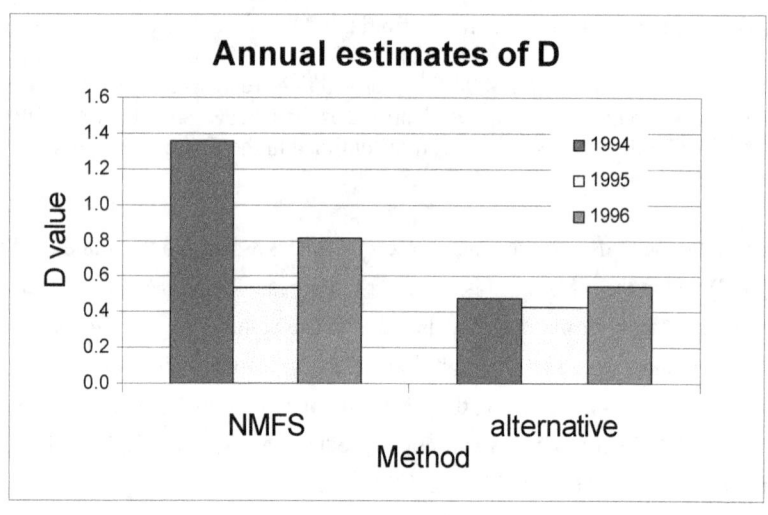

Figure 4. Comparison of 'D' estimates from models using NMFS' set of assumptions and an alternative set of assumptions for all components for the individual years.

Both the NMFS model (Sanford and Smith, 1999), and the IDFG model (Kiefer et al., 1999) produced similar estimates of 'D ' under the same set of assumptions and combinations of transport and inriver groups (Figure 5). For example, the NMFS 94-95 pooled 'D' estimate was 0.84, while the IDFG model 'D' estimates were 0.77 and 0.81. For the following sensitivity analyses, we used only the lower estimate (0.77) based on the example provided by Smith and

Williams (1999). The deviation around the 1:1 line in Figure 5 represents the differences in the two models when all assumptions are the same. Because both models use the same general methods, these deviations are likely due to differences in how fish passage histories were categorized and the inclusion or exclusion of different study groups.

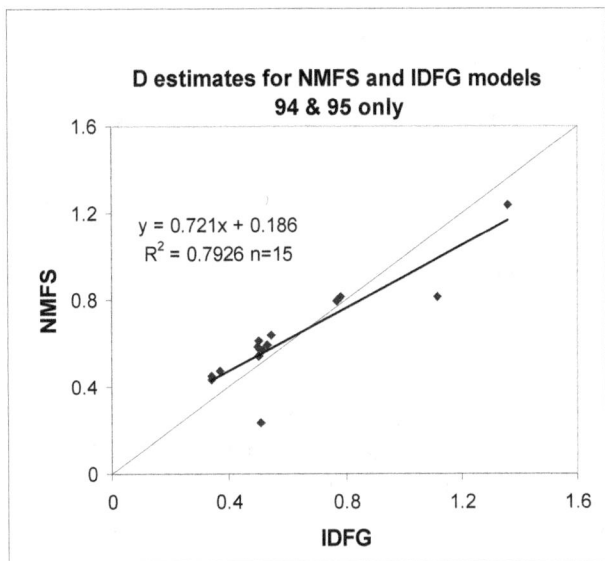

Figure 5: Comparison of 'D' estimates from models created by IDFG and NMFS. Each model run used the same set of assumptions for each of the components used to estimate 'D'.

Sensitivity Analyses

In order to determine which factors have the greatest influence on estimates of 'D', we performed a sensitivity analysis for both the NMFS method and the alternative method by holding all other assumptions fixed.

'D'-values were sensitive to the method used to extrapolate in-river survival rates from the study reach to downstream from BON (Figures 6 and 7). The CJS method produces higher 'D'-value estimates (0.77 NMFS, 0.48 Alternative) compared to estimates that used survival rates generated from the passage models used by PATH (0.18-0.53) (Figure 6).

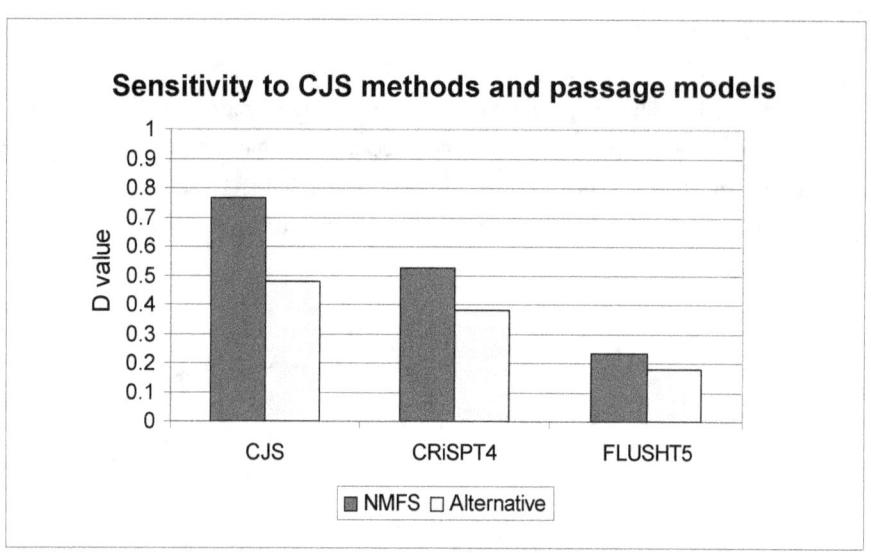

Figure 6. The influence of methods used to expand upper reach survival rate estimates to downriver projects to estimate 'D'. Light colored bars represent NMFS' assumptions and the dark bars represent an alternative set of assumptions, across all categories.

The 'D'-value calculations were also sensitive to the use of per-project expansions versus per-mile expansions (Figure 7). Per-project expanded 'D' estimates were higher than per-mile expanded 'D' estimates, regardless of which data set was used. The calculation of 'D' appears to be relatively insensitive to the method chosen for cohort summary and variance weighting. Both the all-fish-daily data set weighted by the inverse relative variance, and the wild-weekly data set weighted by the inverse relative variance and passage index produced similar results (Figure 7). In addition to the effect of reach survival methods on overall estimates of 'D', the different methods had stronger influence on some of the annual point estimates (Appendix A).

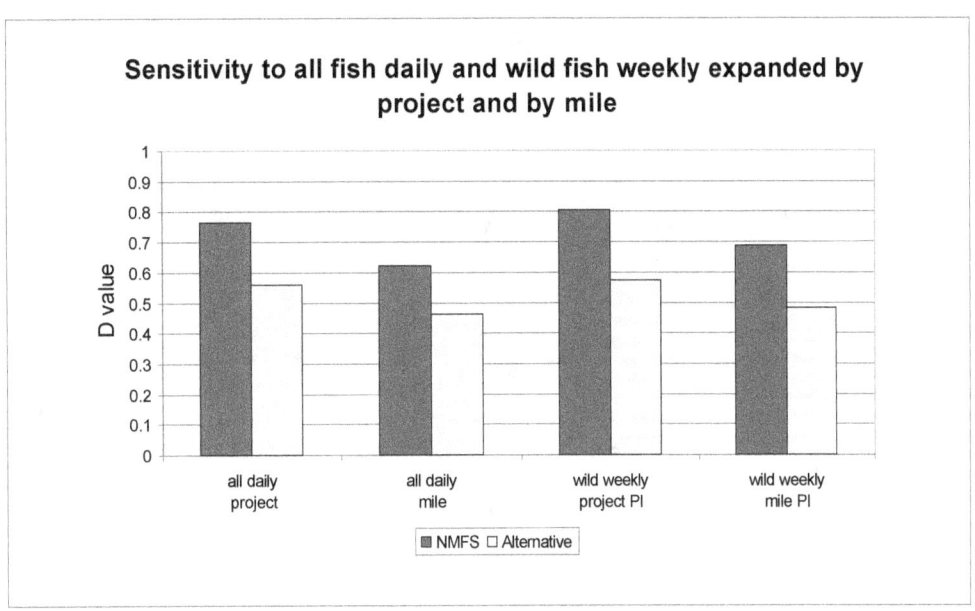

Figure 7. The influence of the different cohorts of PIT-tagged fish used in the CJS recapture model and the method used in the expansion of reach survival rate estimates on the estimates of 'D'. Light colored bars represent NMFS' assumptions across all categories and the dark bars represent an alternative set of assumptions across all categories.

The NMFS approach, of including only the upper two transport locations (LGR and LGO) in the 'D'-value estimate, produced much higher 'D'-values than when all four transport locations were included (Figure 8). When only two transport locations were included, 'D'-values were 0.77 for the NMFS method and 0.71 for the alternative method. When all four transportation locations were included, 'D'-values decreased to 0.46 for the NMFS approach and 0.48 for the alternative approach. The inclusion of three transport locations resulted in intermediate results between those observed for two transport projects and four transport projects. Further, when individual year estimates are considered, the interannual variation in yearly estimates of 'D' shown in Figure 4 appears to be driven largely by the inclusion of only 2 transport projects in 1994 (Figure 9).

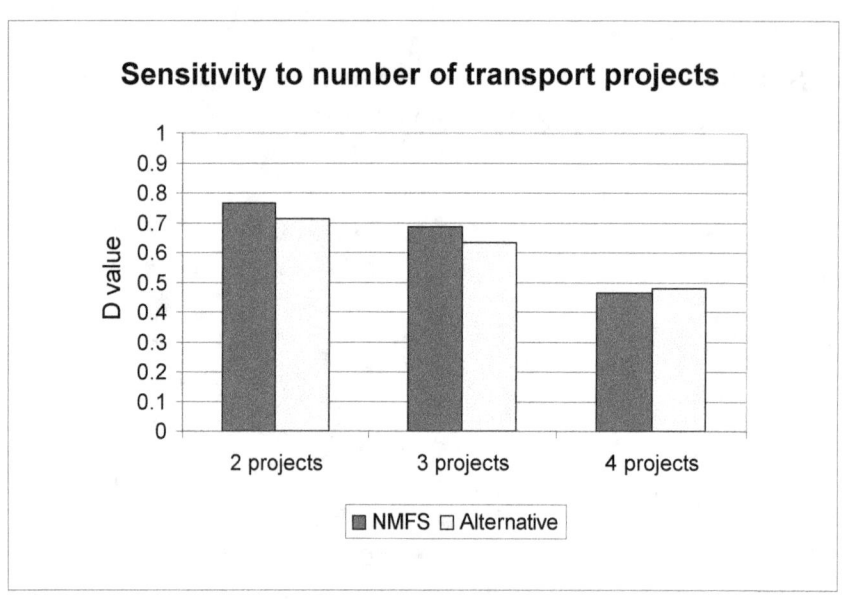

Figure 8. The influence of the number of collector projects used to evaluate transport SARs used to determine estimates of 'D'. Light colored bars represent NMFS' assumptions and the dark bars represent an alternative set of assumptions, across all categories.

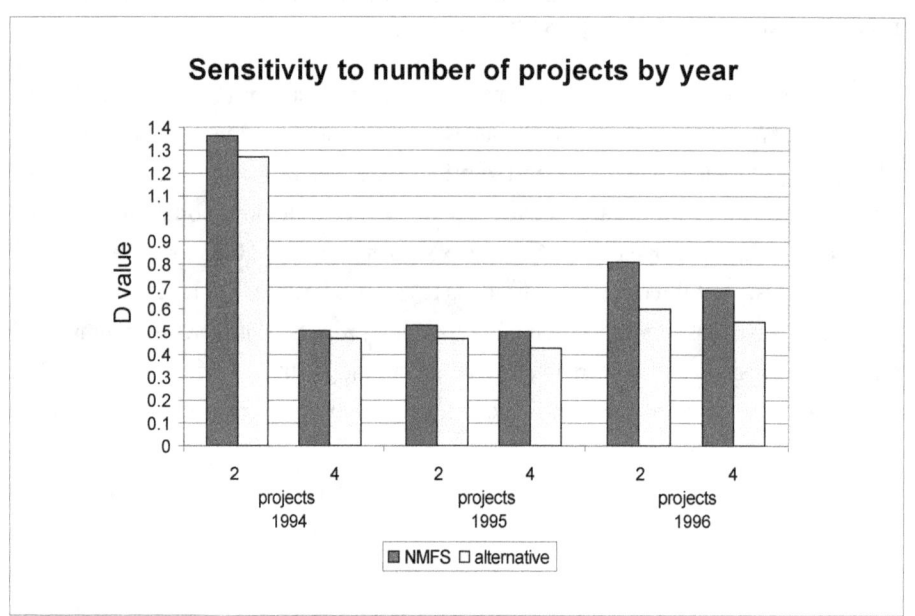

Figure 9. The influence of the number of collector projects used to evaluate transport SARs used to determine estimates of 'D' for individual years. Light colored bars represent NMFS' assumptions and the dark bars represent an alternative set of assumptions, across all categories.

'D'-value estimates were less sensitive to the definition of the in-river groups, and whether bypassed smolts were considered part of the "control" group. When the in-river group included smolts bypassed at LGR and MCN in 1995-1996 (in addition to the non-detected group), 'D'-

values were 0.77 for the NMFS method and 0.48 for the alternative method (Figure 10). When the in-river group included smolts bypassed at MCN in 1995-1996, the 'D'-values were 0.83 and 0.48 respectively. When only the non-detected group was used each year, respective 'D'-values declined to approximately 0.70 and 0.41.

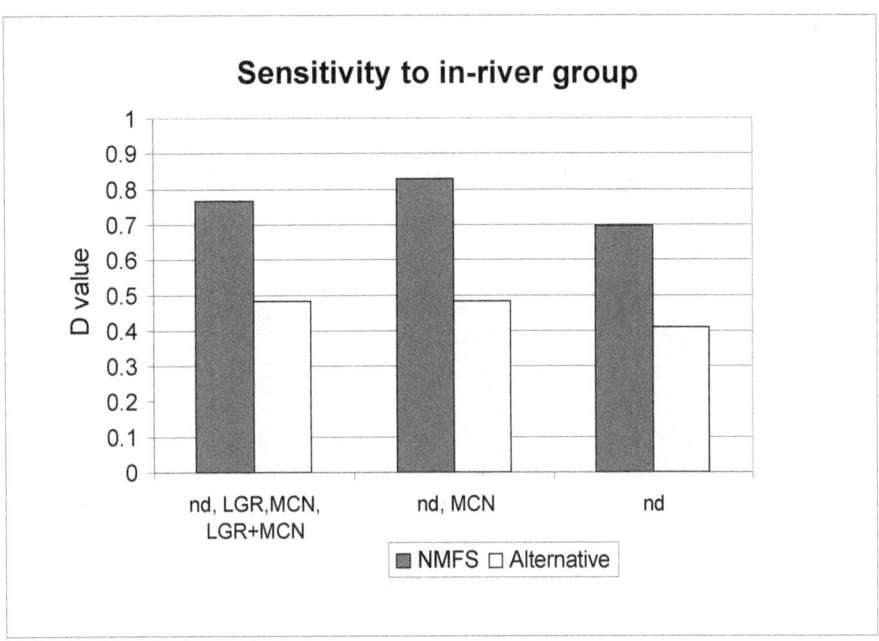

Figure 10. The influence of the number of bypassed projects in-river control fish were detected at in evaluating in-river SARs used to determine estimates of 'D'. Light colored bars represent NMFS' assumptions and the dark bars represent an alternative set of assumptions, across all categories. 'nd' is the non detect group.

'D'-value estimates were relatively insensitive to whether the in-river group included or excluded smolts released at LGR. Using the NMFS method, respective 'D'-values were 0.77 and 0.81 when smolts released at LGR were included and excluded (Figure 1). Using the alternative method, respective 'D'-values were approximately 0.48 and 0.47. Again, while the multi-year results were not sensitive to this factor, individual year estimates were highly variable, depending on the definition of in-river smolts (Appendix A).

The method used to estimate the LGR arrival numbers (to determine numbers of undetected smolts) was not highly influential on 'D'-value estimates. The NMFS 'D'-value was 0.77 when arrival numbers were estimated by NMFS, and 0.78 when arrival numbers were estimated by IDFG. For the alternative method, 'D'-values were 0.48 and 0.52 using NMFS and IDFG arrival numbers, respectively. Estimated 'D'-values for individual years were more sensitive to arrival number estimates than were the multi-year estimates (Appendix A).

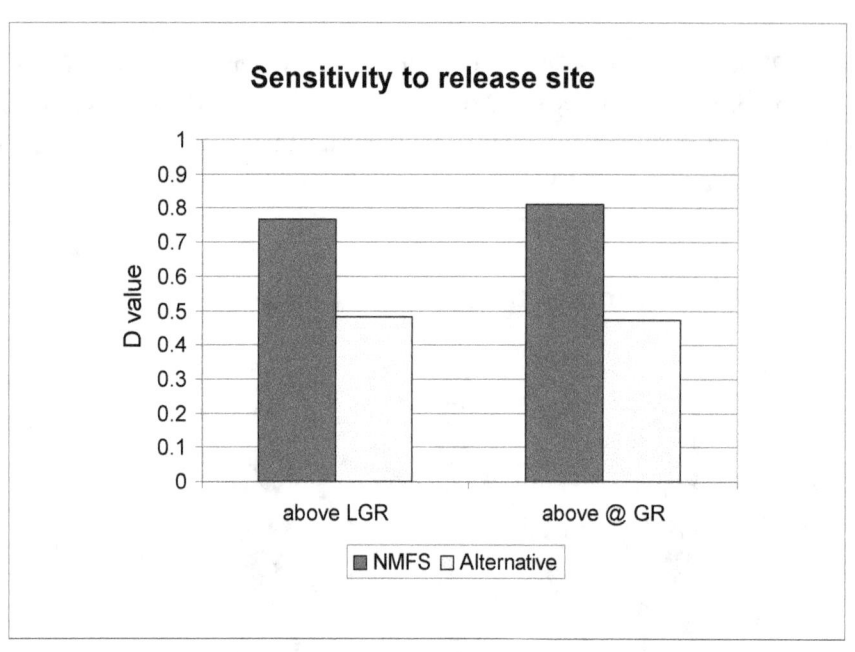

Figure 11. The influence of the release sites used to determine estimates of 'D'. Light colored bars represent NMFS' assumptions across all categories and the dark bars represent an alternative set of assumptions across all categories.

The multi-year estimates were generally insensitive to the inclusion of adult returns from the 1996 smolt migration, and the method of combining years (i. e. pooling adults and estimated smolts to obtain a 'D'-value vs. geometric mean of annual 'D' estimates). This was in part because 1995 and 1996 values were similar (Figure 4). As shown in Figure 12, 'D'-values changed slightly when we included the returns from 1996 (from about 0.77 to 0.80 using the NMFS method with pooled years, and from about 0.85 to 0.84 using the NMFS method and geometric mean). The same pattern was evident, but with much lower 'D'-values, for the alternative method. In this case, adding the 1996 estimates changed 'D' from 0.43 to 0.42 using the pooled years, and from 0.45 to 0.48 using the geometric mean.

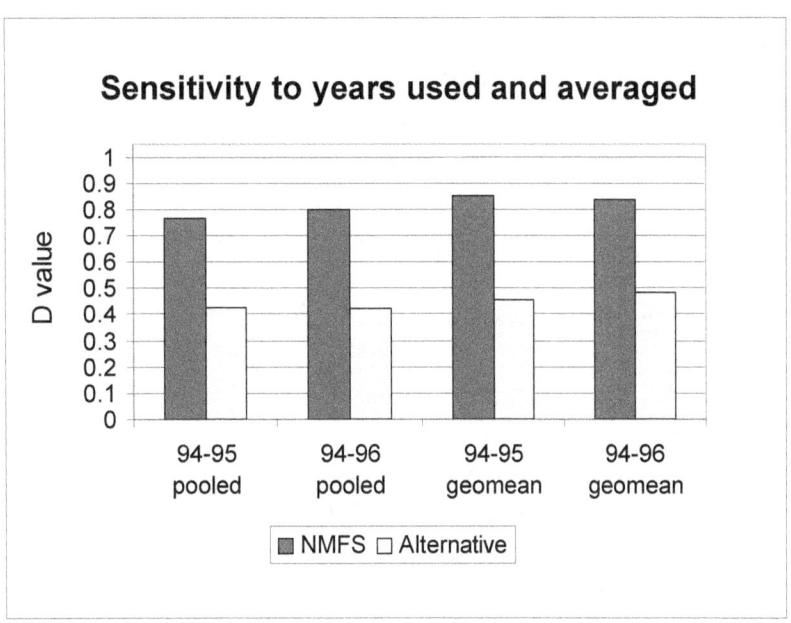

Figure 12. The influence of the years and pooling versus geometric mean (GM) aggregation methods used to determine estimates of 'D'. Light colored bars represent NMFS' assumptions across all categories and the dark bars represent an alternative set of assumptions across all categories.

Evidence of Delayed Mortality

The definition of the study group is highly influential on the 'D'-value estimates, because SARs differ among routes of passage at the dams and among upper vs. lower transportation locations. Sandford and Smith (1999), Kiefer et al. (1999), and NMFS 1994-1996 PIT-tag estimates (Dcalc9496.xls, S. Smith, NMFS) provide evidence of delayed mortality for both in-river and transport groups.

Choice of an appropriate transport group is important in the 'D' estimate, because SARs were greater for smolts transported from the upper two projects (LGR and LGO) than for those transported from the lower projects (LMO and MCN) each year 1994-1996 (Fig. 13a). These SARs (in LGR equivalents) represent first detections for wild chinook PIT-tagged upstream from LGR and transported from these collection/transport sites (Dcalc9496.xls, S. Smith, NMFS). This pattern, in part, provides evidence of delayed mortality for non-bypassed smolts since all groups were collected only once (for transportation). Apparently the A-Fish considered transportation only from the upper two dams, and therefore the A-Fish 'D'-values are biased upward, compared to the population at large.

Choice of a representative in-river (control group) is also influential on 'D', because SARs vary according to the number of times a smolt is bypassed. The A-Fish (Fig. 5.4.3.2-1), Sandford and Smith (1999), Kiefer et al. (1999), and the NMFS 1994-1996 estimates also provide evidence that SARs decreased when the number of times fish were bypassed increased (Fig. 13b). Point estimates of SARs (in LGR equivalents) were consistently higher each year for those fish that were not bypassed at any of the four, collector projects (0X). Point estimates of SARs were intermediate for smolts bypassed one (1X) and two times (2X). Few to no adults returned from fish collected and bypassed three (3X) and four times (4X), although sample sizes were small (fewer than 5,000 total) for these groups.

If SARs are influenced by hydrosystem migration route, the above pattern of decreasing survival rates with multiple bypass is opposite of the expected pattern based on PATH direct survival rates estimates. The expected pattern is that survival rate should increase the more times a fish is bypassed since these fish avoid turbine mortality. PATH used direct survival rate estimates of 0.98, 0.90 and 0.98 for passage through collection/bypass systems, turbines and spillway routes, respectively, in the spring/summer chinook analyses. Based on these rates, fish that experienced collection/bypass four times (4X) would have a direct survival rate at the dams of 0.92 (0.98^4) under all spill conditions. (Note: this example represents only cumulative passage survival rate at the four dams; reservoir survival rate was excluded). In contrast, survival rate through 4 dams for uncollected smolts would be 0.66 (0.90^4) under no-spill conditions, and 0.76 ($[0.9*0.6 + 0.98*0.4]^4$) when 40% of smolts are spilled at each project (Fig. 13c). Reconciling the difference between the patterns in SARs and direct passage survival rates, leads to the conclusion that hydro-related delayed mortality exists, at least for collected and bypassed smolts.

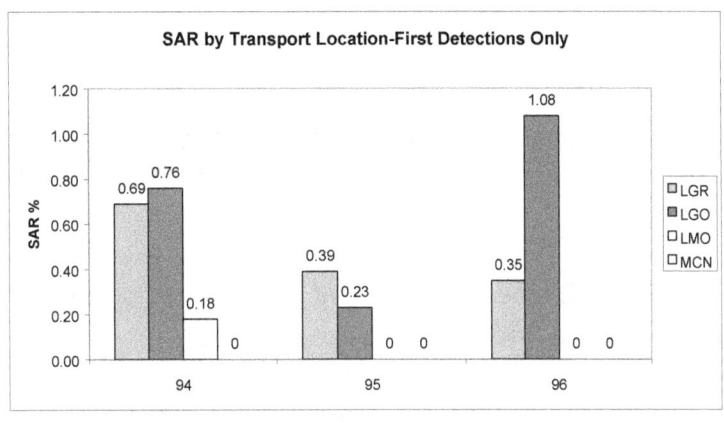

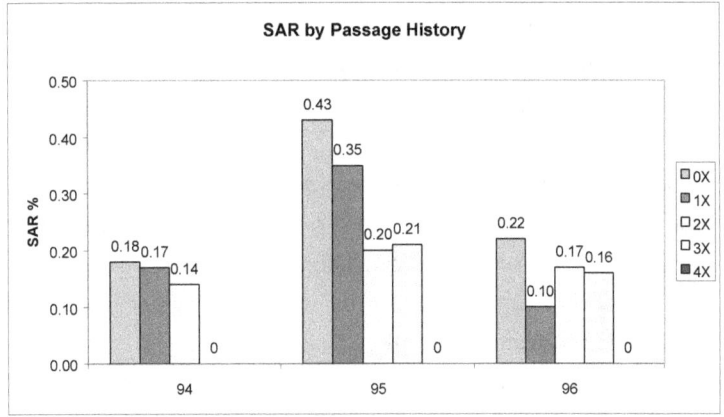

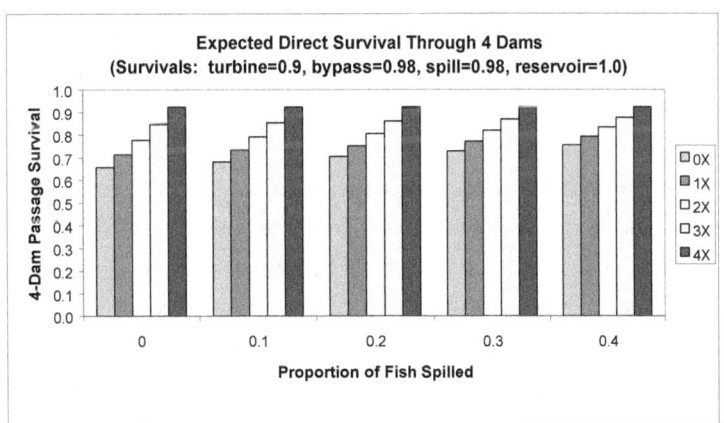

Figure 13. Estimated smolt-to-adult return rates (SAR) for transported wild spring/summer chinook released above LGR and first detected at the respective collection/transport dams, 1994-1996 (upper panel, 13a); SAR of wild spring/summer chinook by in-river passage history: non-detected (0X), and bypassed one, two, three and four times (1X, 2X, 3X and 4X, respectively), 1994-1996 (middle panel, 13b); and expected dam passage survival rate through four dams for passage history groups 0X, 1X, 2X, 3X, and 4X, based on direct survival rate estimates of 0.90 for turbine passage, 0.98 for bypass and spillway passage (lower panel, 13c).

DISCUSSION

In the A-Fish, NMFS suggests that transportation effectiveness of spring/summer chinook may have improved markedly in recent years, based on estimates of 'D'-values (differential delayed mortality) for 1994-1995. NMFS suggested that if 'D' is high (estimated in A-Fish at > 0.8), there may be partial support for delaying a decision on hydropower options for Snake River salmon and steelhead. That is, if 'D' is high **and** extra mortality of in-river and transported smolts is unrelated to the hydropower system, transportation options may meet recovery standards as well or better than natural river options. NMFS further suggested that studies could reduce the uncertainty about true values of 'D' and provide greater confidence to make a decision on the alternative management action needed to recover listed Snake River spring/summer chinook. In this analysis, we demonstrate that it is unlikely that 'D' is high. In addition, we present evidence that the extra mortality of in-river fish is related to the hydrosystem.

We estimated recent 'D's across what we believe was a reasonable range of assumptions based on the recent PIT tag data. Based on our analysis of the 1994-1996 PIT tag data, there is a wide range of possible 'D'-values, with the NMFS' estimate falling at the upper end of this distribution (~90th to 95th percentile). Our analysis demonstrates that recent estimates of 'D' from PIT-tag studies have a wide distribution centered about 0.48 (geometric mean), when considering the suite of assumptions that determine how 'D' is calculated. The NMFS 'D' estimate of ~0.8 is higher than most of the 'D's estimated under what we consider to be a reasonable set of assumptions. Based on alternative sets of assumptions and data groupings that we believe are more reasonable and conservative, the recent PIT tag data suggest 0.48 is a more likely estimate of 'D' than 0.8.

In this paper, we also demonstrate that 'D' is a model estimate that cannot be measured and that some of the key uncertainties and assumptions are unlikely to be resolved. NMFS concludes in the A-Fish (NMFS, 1999) that the key issue in the "1999 Decision" concerns the risk of delaying to resolve the uncertainty about transportation mortality (or 'D'-values) and the primary causes of extra mortality. NMFS states that research is already underway for directly estimating transportation mortality, and adequate data should be forthcoming within less than 10 years. However, they also recognize that while research regarding sources of extra mortality may begin to yield useful information in as few as 5 years, ultimately, such research is likely to require 10 to 20 years before major reductions in uncertainty are realized.

We have focussed here on point estimates, but the confidence intervals estimated for 'D' (using fixed assumptions) are large (A-Fish section 5.4.3.1). The true confidence intervals would be much wider than reported if variance from other models (e.g., CJS estimates) and assumptions (e.g., expansions and study groups) were also incorporated. Recent SARs from all routes of in-river passage and transportation are much less than that required to achieve survival and recovery goals, and wild populations have continued to decline. The small numbers of wild smolts and low SARs both contribute to wide confidence intervals and pose experimental design problems needed to reduce these uncertainties. For example, small sample size hampers estimating reach survival rate and SARs for a non-detected group. It remains unclear whether or how we will resolve the methods for obtaining an empirical estimate of 'D' using a true control group if SARs do not improve.

NMFS asserts from the A-Fish that *"Ongoing direct experiments that contrast the return rates of tagged fish that pass through the hydrosystem versus the return rates of transported fish can resolve this question in a clear and unambiguous manner"*. This statement echoes advice given as early as 1975 when Collins et al. (1975) stated *"Analysis of the test-to-control ratios provides the best insight to the benefit possible from the transportation system, but total percentage to return obtained from the groups transported must also be examined to accurately assess the effectiveness of the system as it now operates"*. Indeed, these studies have been conducted since 1968. We believe that more data are unlikely to perfect our understanding of 'D' or eliminate the uncertainty in the most influential assumptions. 'D' is not a measurement; it is a model value, which is sensitive to many assumptions and the definition of transport and in-river groups. While a few components of the 'D'-value estimate are measurable (input data) and computation differences between the models can be resolved, the sensitivity analysis here highlights the assumptions and uncertainties that are not likely to be resolved in the near term. We caution that the model we used to estimate 'D' for this sensitivity analysis is not identical to the NMFS model; nevertheless, the two models show the same basic pattern of sensitivity to assumptions.

Certain combinations of assumptions can have a great effect in estimating 'D'. In addition, in some cases, single assumptions also have a large effect on annual estimates of 'D'. 'D' estimates were most sensitive to the number of projects from which fish were transported downstream of LGR. In 1994, under both sets of assumptions, the 'D'-value estimated using four collection projects was much lower than two collection projects. However, in 1995 and 1996 the difference in 'D' using two and four collection projects was not as dramatic in 1994. Therefore, the estimated high 'D'-values are mainly driven for this single assumption for one year (Figure 9).

We believe the assumptions used to calculate 'D' should either reflect the hydrosystem operations invoked in any given year or transport operations proposed for the future. If in any year, fish were transported from projects downstream of LGR and LGO, then we believe these fish should be included in estimates of 'D'. In 1994, greater than 80% of the fish that entered the MCN bypass system were transported. However, even if this proportion were much lower, when all transport projects are included in the analysis, the annual SAR_T would be appropriately influenced by the number of fish transported. Further, for proposed transport-based management actions, the current transportation configuration (PATH --A1) and the configuration where transportation is maximized (PATH --A2) will include collection and transportation at three and four projects, respectively. Therefore, based on past and future transportation operations, it is unclear why fish transported at the lower two projects were excluded from the NMFS analysis.

The method used to expand survival estimates from study reaches to the entire migratory corridor has a large influence on the estimate of 'D'. NMFS estimates an annual reach survival rate using a CJS mark recapture model using wild and hatchery daily released PIT-tagged fish. Other mark-recapture methods produced similar survival rates over the upper reaches (Table 2). These CJS methods are likely the most accurate estimate of survival rates over these smaller reaches in years where mark-recapture studies were conducted. However, there are several methods for expanding these survival rate estimates to the entire hydrosystem. These methods can greatly affect the estimated number of smolts arriving at BON used to calculate a BON SAR_C . The simplest approach is to calculate a per- project survival rate value from the study reach and expand this by the number of projects, as employed by NMFS. This assumes that smolt experience similar mortality at all projects despite the great differences in time spent in reservoirs and the high variability in predator numbers. Lower projects generally have higher predator numbers and are much longer than upper reservoirs (i.e. JDA is longer than all four Snake River reservoirs combined). Expanding reach survival rates by mile generally produces a higher mortality for the lower project as these projects are generally longer. Passage models more explicitly account for difference in predators and environmental conditions (as in CRiSP) or for cumulative mortality expressed the longer a smolt remains in the hydrosystem (FLUSH). Passage models are calibrated to many years of data and are more general in their predictions. CJS methods are specific to a given year. Therefore, CJS estimates may produce more accurate estimates of survival rates in the years and over the reaches the survival rate studies were conducted whereas, the passage models may be more accurate in extrapolating to years and sites over which studies are lacking. Both methods are supportable but depend on their application.

Our analysis suggests that under all sets of assumptions examined approximately 10% of the calculated 'D'-values exceeded 0.8. If 'D' is 0.8 then the transport delayed mortality is lower than previously suggested in the PATH decision analysis. This difference alone however, would not alter the conclusions of the PATH analysis that suggest that dam breaching is the only management action that has a high likelihood of achieving recovery of these stocks. Because 'D' and extra mortality are both components of delayed mortality, the mortality no longer explained by a high 'D' is absorb by the extra mortality component. If extra mortality is related to the hydrosystem then a high 'D' with the a higher hydrosystem extra mortality will give same results of achieving recovery goals for transport based options as a lower 'D' and lower hydrosystem extra mortality. Transport options lead to recovery only when 'D' is high and the source of extra mortality is not related to the experience during hydrosystem passage. Therefore, only under certain assumptions of the source of extra mortality and a high 'D' value will transportation-based management actions be as effective as breaching at leading to recovery of listed Snake River stocks (A-Fish Figure 5.5.1.4-3).

The extra mortality hypotheses pursued in the A-Fish and PATH are 1) ocean regime shift, 2) reduced stock viability (formerly know as the BKD hypothesis), and 3) the hydrosystem. All hypotheses must explain why post-BON mortality of Snake River stocks is greater than for stocks migrating through three or fewer dams (in order to be consistent with the greater observed declines in the Snake River stocks since the completion of the Snake River dams). Evidence of the source of extra mortality is limited. The ocean regime hypothesis suggests that ocean conditions have become less favorable for upstream stocks than downstream stocks since the mid-1970's and may soon become equally favorable for all stocks. Because upstream and downstream stocks overlap spatially in the ocean, the mechanism explaining this differential ocean impacts is unclear. The reduced stock viability hypothesis suggests that BKD, negative interactions with hatchery fish (hatchery fish production has increased to mitigate for losses to dams), and genetic degradation has increased for upstream stocks independent but coincidentally during the development and operation of the hydrosystem. Evidence suggests that BKD is equally prevalent in upstream and downstream stocks (IDFG 1998). Little evidence exists for the other proposed mechanisms. The hydrosystem extra-mortality hypothesis suggests that cumulative stress from hydrosystem experience results in a decreased ability for upstream stocks to survive below BON than downstream stocks. This analysis and the A-Fish provide evidence for hydrosystem extra mortality.

Hydrosystem extra mortality is evident when comparing in-river "controls" with different bypass histories, and transported fish collected from a different number of projects. Smolts that are collected/bypassed a number of times have a lower SAR than smolts that are not bypassed (true in-river fish), resulting in an upward bias in 'D' (Figure 13 b). Similarly, when LMO and MCN transport groups are excluded, the transport SAR is inflated, causing an upward bias in 'D' (Figure 13a). This empirical evidence provides support for the hydrosystem extra mortality hypothesis and illustrates how the added extra mortality increases 'D'.

From a biological perspective, hydrosystem delayed mortality is expected due to the cumulative stresses of hydrosystem passage, including the collection/bypass systems (*see* discussions of the hydro extra mortality hypothesis in Marmorek and Peters 1998a and b). Consider, for instance, that when surface-oriented smolts approach a dam, they are delayed (S. Pettit, IDFG, personal communication). As the water current pulls smolts downward toward the turbine intakes, radio tag studies show that smolts fight the current. From the intake screens, the guided smolts are returned in 3 seconds back to the surface (about 70 feet) into a turbulent gatewell. Smolts go from 1, to 3, and back to 1 atmospheric pressures in about 10 seconds. At LGR they are then piped from the gallery nearly a quarter mile to below the dam at high velocity (30 ft/second) and pressure through two 90-degree turns, experiencing high turbulence and rapid deceleration at the end. Smolts are then de-watered and passed through a separator (USACE, 1981). Typically for transport evaluations, smolts are then held in raceways up to 48 hours, dip-netted and transferred to the sample room, anesthetized and marked, returned to the raceways for recovery, then barged, trucked, or flushed through an 8-inch pipe for release to the river. In recent bypass/collection operations at the dams (since 1994), bypassed smolts may avoid the raceway holding and handling, but experience the same stressors up to the point of diversion. The above description is for passage through one of eight dams. Given that stress has cumulative effects (e.g., Adams, et al., 1985; Bjornn et al., 1984-87; Vaughn et al., 1984; Wedemeyer et al., 1990; and Submission 20 of Marmorek and Peters, 1998b), the hypothesis of delayed mortality of in-river and transported smolts due to hydrosystem passage has a strong biological, as well as empirical, basis.

While hydrosystem delayed mortality may have an empirical and theoretical basis, what is important in terms of 'D' is why this mortality is greater for transported fish than for non-transported fish (i.e. 'D' < 1). The above description of the experience of a bypassed/collected fish is most relevant to transported fish at collection projects because most of the fish entering the bypass/collection system at these projects are subsequently transported. All transported fish are subjected to this experience which is not true for in-river smolts which may be bypassed, go through turbines, or over the spillway. In addition, transported smolts are subjected to the stress of crowding and injury during transport. High levels of descaling have been reported for transported fish (Williams and Mathews 1995; Basham and Garrett 1996). Stress, injury, and crowding may trigger disease outbreak (e.g., BKD, fungal infection) and lead to delayed mortality. The physiological state and time of saltwater entry may also be poorly synchronized for transported groups. For example, Fagurlund et al. (1995) cite studies of effects of premature saltwater entry (incomplete smoltification) with coho salmon, resulting in high mortality, and, in many of the survivors, a reduction in or cessation of growth. These factors may be responsible for the higher delayed mortality experience by transported fish as suggested by a 'D' value consistently less than 1.

NMFS draws several conclusions in the A-Fish (Sec. 10-6) regarding balancing uncertainties with actions. They acknowledged that if all assumptions are weighted equally and PATH estimates of delayed mortality are used, breaching is clearly much more likely than current operations to meet survival and recovery population thresholds. However, if PATH prospective models are run assuming only higher 'D'-values (minimal differential delayed mortality due to transportation), this difference and the advantages to breaching are substantially reduced and may even disappear under certain assumptions about extra mortality. Based on these analyses, it appears unlikely that the recent 'D' values are higher than those used in the PATH analysis. The range of 'D' value estimated in this analyses were considered in the PATH analyses. Specifically the CRiSP prospective weighted average for 'D' was 0.67 and the FLUSH prospective value for 'D' was 0.48. These weighted and unweighted results from PATH, for these 'D' values, did not yield recovery for transport based options (A1 and A2).

While NMFS accurately reported the PATH conclusion in the A-Fish that the natural-river options were most likely to achieve survival and recovery standards for listed salmon and steelhead, and were least risky across a broad range of uncertainties, their 'D'-value sensitivity focussed on a narrow, optimistic range of 'D's, and dismissed hydropower-related delayed mortality. However, in terms of management consequences, even if 'D' is assumed to be high, when combined with hydrosystem extra (delayed) mortality, the natural river option is clearly better than transportation options (A-Fish). Transportation options perform nearly as well as (or better than) natural river options **only** when extra mortality is hypothesized to be unrelated to the hydropower system, and 'D' is high (greater than 0.8). NMFS suggested that decisions might be delayed to recover listed salmon, in order to study what the "true" 'D'-value might be. Simply studying 'D', if that were possible, without determining the source of extra mortality, yields little additional insight into effects of the different actions. Given the past performance and dangerously low levels of these stocks, decisions of future management actions to recover these fish should based be conservative assessments of the efficacy of past and current management actions.

ACKNOWLEDGEMENTS

We thank Larry Basham, Tom Berggren, Henry Franzoni and Sergei Rasskazov of the Fish Passage Center for their efforts in gathering raw data for our analyses. We also would like to thank Paul Bunn and Alan Byrne of the Idaho Department of Fish and Game, for generously sharing with us their model and results of earlier analyses of delayed mortality.

LITERATURE CITED

Adams, S.M., Breck, J.E., and McLean, R.B. 1985. Cumulative stress-induced mortality of gizzard shad in southeastern U.S. Reservoir. Environmental Biology of Fishes 13:103-112.

Basham, L. and L. Garrett. 1996. Historical review of juvenile fish descaling information collected at the Columbia and Snake River transportation projects. Section 8.3 in Marmorek, D. I.P. Parnell, and D. Bouillon (ed.). 1996. Plan for Analyzing and Testing Hypotheses (PATH); preliminary report on retrospective analyses. March 15, 1996. Compiled and edited by ESSA Technologies, Ltd., Vancouver, B.C.

Bjornn, T.C., Congleton, J.L., Ringe, R.R., and Moffitt, C.M. 1984-87. Survival rate of chinook salmon smolts as related to stress at dams and smolt quality. Idaho Cooperative Fish and Wildlife Research Unit. Tech. Repts. 85-1, 87-4, and 88-1. Moscow, Idaho.

Collins, G. B., W. J. Ebel, G. E. Monan, H. L. Raymond, and G. K. Tanonaka. 1975. The Snake River Salmon Steelhead Crisis: Its Relation to Dams and the National Energy Crisis. Northwest Fisheries Center Processed Report, February 1975.

Fagerlund, U.H.M., J.R. McBride and I.V. Williams. 1995. Stress and Tolerance. Chapter 8 in: C. Groot, L. Margolis and W.C. Clarke (ed.). 1995. Physiological Ecology of Pacific Salmon. 1995. UBC Press, Vancouver, Canada.

Kiefer, R., Bunn P., and Nemeth, D. 1999 draft manuscript. Snake River chinook salmon smolt-to-adult return rate comparisons by mainstem migration route. Draft. Idaho Department of Fish and Game, Boise, ID 83707.

Marmorek, D.R., and Peters, C.N. (eds.). 1998a. Plan for Analyzing and Testing Hypotheses (PATH): Preliminary decision analysis report on Snake River spring/summer chinook. Draft Report, March 1998. ESSA Technologies Ltd., Vancouver, B.C., Canada. 92pp. + appendices.

Marmorek, D.R., and Peters, C.N. (eds.). 1998b. Plan for Analyzing and Testing Hypotheses (PATH): Weight of Evidence Report. August 21, 1998. Compiled and edited by ESSA Technologies Ltd., Vancouver, B.C., Canada. 116pp. + appendices.

Marmorek, D.R., Peters, C.N., and I. Parnell (eds.). 1998. Plan for Analyzing and Testing Hypotheses (PATH): Final Report for Fiscal Year 1998 December 16, 1998. Compiled and edited by ESSA Technologies Ltd., Vancouver, B.C., Canada. 263pp.

NMFS (National Marine Fisheries Service). 1999. An assessment of Lower Snake River hydrosystem alternatives on survival and recovery of Snake River salmonids. Appendix __ to the U.S. Army Corps of Engineers' Lower Snake River Juvenile Salmonid Migration Feasibility Study. 163pp. + appendices.

Sandford, B.P. and Smith, S.G. 1999 manuscript. Smolt-to-adult return percentages for Snake River basin salmonids. Northwest Fisheries Science Center, National Marine Fisheries Service, 2725 Montlake Blvd. East, Seattle, WA 98112.

Smith, S.G. 1999. NMFS Methods for Estimating Survival through the Hydrosystem 1966-1980 and 1993-1998. Memorandum to Chris Toole, NMFS, Portland, Oregon and distributed to the PATH Planning Group on 11 March 1999. 11pp.

Smith, S.G., and Williams J.G. 1999. Memorandum from NMFS responding to State and Tribes' request for information on NMFS analyses regarding 'D' analyses, June 1999.

U.S. Army Corps of Engineers (USACE). 1981. North Pacific Division Fish Facilities Manual. Prepared by U.S. Army Corps of Engineers, Portland District, Fish and Wildlife Section. March 1981. 141pp.

Vaughn, D.S., Yoshiyama, R.M., Breck, J.E., and DeAngelis, D.L. 1984. Modeling approaches for assessing the effects of stress on fish populations. *In* Cairns et al. 1984. Containment Effects on Fisheries. Wiley: Toronto, Canada. Pg. 259-278.

Wedemeyer, G.A., Barton, B.A., and Mcleay, D.J. 1990. Stress and acclimation. *In* Methods for Fish Biology. American Fisheries Society: Bethesda, Maryland. Pg. 451-489.

White G.C. 1999. Program MARK. Department of Fish and Wildlife. Colorado State University, Fort Collins, Colorado.

Williams, J.G. and G.M. Matthews. 1995. A review of flow and survival relationships for spring and summer chinook salmon, *Oncorhynchus tshawytscha*, from the Snake River Basin. Fish. Bull. 93: 732-740.

Appendix A

Detailed data summaries of estimated 'D'-values developed for:

A response by State, Tribal, and USFWS technical staff to the 'D' analyses and discussion in the Anadromous Fish Appendix to the U.S. Army Corps of Engineers' Lower Snake River Juvenile Salmonid Migration Feasibility Study

Appendix A includes two tables. Table 1 presents a description of the methods used and the grouping of runs performed for each category of data set to estimate 'D'-values. Table 2 presents the detailed outputs ('D'-values of each run by category and method).

Eight methods are based on various combinations of how we determine V_c. We grouped methods by the assumption about reach expansion (by project or mile), cohort method (daily or weekly time accounts), rearing type (wild or hatchery and wild fish combined), weighting method, and by reach survival rate estimate (CJS or PATH models).

The 27 runs per category are arranged by in-river detection group, number of transportation sites, release groups, and migration year. The in-river detection groups include combinations of fish never detected, fish bypassed at McNary Dam, fish bypassed at Lower Granite Dam, fish bypassed at Little Goose Dam, fish bypassed at both Lower Granite and McNary dams, etc. Transportation sites are grouped as two-site (Lower Granite and Little Goose collection facilities) or four-site (Lower Granite, Little Goose, Lower Monumental, and McNary collection facilities). Release sites are grouped as either smolts released above Lower Granite Dam only, or smolts released above and at Lower Granite Dam. Not all combinations of in-river detection, transportation sites, and release groups apply to every migration year (e.g., there were no bypass detection groups for 1994).

'D'-value results are presented for each run of a method category (Table 2). In addition, we provide geometric mean and pooled 'D'-values for eight groupings of the individual runs. Estimates are provided by migration path (transported or in-river passage) of the below-Bonneville Dam juveniles and Lower Granite Dam adult returns associated with the given juvenile migration year and model run. Adult and smolt counts used for estimation of 'D'-values for each set of assumptions or data categories are presented.

Appendix Table 1

METHOD

Category hatchery/wild	cohort method	reach expansion		
1 all (both)	daily	project		NMFS arrival #
2 all (both)	daily	mile		NMFS arrival #
3 wild	weekly	project (PI)	PI	NMFS arrival #
4 wild	weekly	mile (PI)	PI	NMFS arrival #
5 CRiSPT5				NMFS arrival #
6 CRiSPT4				
7 FLUSHT5				NMFS arrival #
8 FLUSHT4				NMFS arrival #
9 all (both)	daily	project		IDFG arrival #
10 wild	weekly	mile (PI)	PI	IDFG arrival #

GROUPINGS

Run #	Year	Above/At LGR	Transport	In-River
1	94	above	lgr, lgo	undetect
2	95	above	lgr, lgo	undetect
3	96	above	lgr, lgo	undetect
4	94	above	lgr, lgo, lmn	undetect
5	95	above	lgr, lgo, lmn	undetect
6	96	above	lgr, lgo, lmn	undetect
7	94	above	lgr, lgo, lmn, mcn	undetect
8	95	above	lgr, lgo, lmn, mcn	undetect
9	96	above	lgr, lgo, lmn, mcn	undetect
10	95	above	lgr, lgo	undetect, mcn bypass only
11	96	above	lgr, lgo	undetect, mcn bypass only
12	95	above	lgr, lgo, lmn	undetect, mcn bypass only
13	96	above	lgr, lgo, lmn	undetect, mcn bypass only
14	95	above	lgr, lgo, lmn, mcn	undetect, mcn bypass only
15	96	above	lgr, lgo, lmn, mcn	undetect, mcn bypass only
16	95	above	lgr, lgo	undetect, lgr, mcn, lgrmcn
17	96	above	lgr, lgo	undetect, lgr, mcn, lgrmcn
18	95	above	lgr, lgo, lmn	undetect, lgr, mcn, lgrmcn
19	96	above	lgr, lgo, lmn	undetect, lgr, mcn, lgrmcn
20	95	above	lgr, lgo, lmn, mcn	undetect, lgr, mcn, lgrmcn
21	96	above	lgr, lgo, lmn, mcn	undetect, lgr, mcn, lgrmcn
22	95	above and at	lgr, lgo	undetect, lgr, mcn, lgrmcn
23	96	above and at	lgr, lgo	undetect, lgr, mcn, lgrmcn
24	95	above and at	lgr, lgo, lmn	undetect, lgr, mcn, lgrmcn
25	96	above and at	lgr, lgo, lmn	undetect, lgr, mcn, lgrmcn
26	95	above and at	lgr, lgo, lmn, mcn	undetect, lgr, mcn, lgrmcn
27	96	above and at	lgr, lgo, lmn, mcn	undetect, lgr, mcn, lgrmcn

Appendix Table 2

All fish, daily, per-project survival expansion, NMFS arrivals

Run	Year	Transpor	Groups	In-river	D-value	94-96 Geom	94-95 Geom	94-96 Pooled	94-95 Pooled	BBsmolt Transpo	BBsmolt Inriver	Adults Transpo	Adults Inriver
1	94	2 trans	above lgr	no detect	1.360	0.726	0.712	0.715	0.697	1520	1241	10	6
2	95	2 trans	above lgr	no detect	0.373					2227	934	8	9
3	96	2 trans	above lgr	no detect	0.755					431	814	2	5
4	94	3 trans	above lgr	no detect	1.114	0.641	0.618	0.636	0.618	2042	1241	11	6
5	95	3 trans	above lgr	no detect	0.343					2419	934	8	9
6	96	3 trans	above lgr	no detect	0.689					472	814	2	5
7	94	4 trans	above lgr	no detect	0.508	0.491	0.416	0.424	0.398	4479	1241	11	6
8	95	4 trans	above lgr	no detect	0.341					2439	934	8	9
9	96	4 trans	above lgr	no detect	0.682					477	814	2	5
	94	2 trans	above lgr	no detect	1.360	0.830	0.861	0.817	0.828	1520	1241	10	6
10	95	2 trans	above lgr	no detect, mcn	0.545					2227	1518	8	10
11	96	2 trans	above lgr	no detect, mcn	0.770					431	997	2	6
	94	3 trans	above lgr	no detect	1.114	0.733	0.748	0.727	0.734	2042	1241	11	6
12	95	3 trans	above lgr	no detect, mcn	0.502					2419	1518	8	10
13	96	3 trans	above lgr	no detect, mcn	0.703					472	997	2	6
	94	4 trans	above lgr	no detect	0.508	0.561	0.503	0.485	0.474	4479	1241	11	6
14	95	4 trans	above lgr	no detect, mcn	0.498					2439	1518	8	10
15	96	4 trans	above lgr	no detect, mcn	0.696					477	997	2	6
	94	2 trans	above lgr	no detect	1.360	0.837	0.851	0.797	0.766	1520	1241	10	6
16	95	2 trans	above lgr	no detect, mcn, lgr, lgr/mcn	0.532					2529	2841	9	19
17	96	2 trans	above lgr	no detect, mcn, lgr, lgr/mcn	0.809					517	1464	2	7
	94	3 trans	above lgr	no detect	1.114	0.735	0.757	0.712	0.685	2042	1241	11	6
18	95	3 trans	above lgr	no detect, mcn, lgr, lgr/mcn	0.514					3200	2841	11	19
19	96	3 trans	above lgr	no detect, mcn, lgr, lgr/mcn	0.694					603	1464	2	7
	94	4 trans	above lgr	no detect	0.508	0.558	0.504	0.497	0.463	4479	1241	11	6
20	95	4 trans	above lgr	no detect, mcn, lgr, lgr/mcn	0.501					3285	2841	11	19
21	96	4 trans	above lgr	no detect, mcn, lgr, lgr/mcn	0.684					612	1464	2	7
	94	2 trans	above & @ lgr	no detect	1.360	0.774	1.031	0.771	0.811	1520	1241	10	6
22	95	2 trans	above & @ lgr	no detect, mcn, lgr, lgr/mcn	0.781					28398	9036	108	44
23	96	2 trans	above & @ lgr	no detect, mcn, lgr, lgr/mcn	0.437					8682	3791	11	11
	94	3 trans	above & @ lgr	no detect	1.114	0.714	0.927	0.758	0.793	2042	1241	11	6
24	95	3 trans	above & @ lgr	no detect, mcn, lgr, lgr/mcn	0.771					30365	9036	114	44
25	96	3 trans	above & @ lgr	no detect, mcn, lgr, lgr/mcn	0.423					8953	3791	11	11
	94	4 trans	above & @ lgr	no detect	0.508	0.548	0.625	0.714	0.735	4479	1241	11	6
26	95	4 trans	above & @ lgr	no detect, mcn, lgr, lgr/mcn	0.768					30486	9036	114	44
27	96	4 trans	above & @ lgr	no detect, mcn, lgr, lgr/mcn	0.423					8967	3791	11	11

All fish, daily, per-mile survival expansion, NMFS arrivals

Run	Year	Transpor	Groups	In-river	D-value	94-96 Geom	94-95 Geom	94-96 Pooled	94-95 Pooled	BBsmolt Transpo	BBsmolt Inriver	Adults Transpo	Adults Inriver
1	94	2 trans	above lgr	no detect	1.071	0.589	0.554	0.577	0.542	1520	977	10	6
2	95	2 trans	above lgr	no detect	0.286					2227	717	8	9
3	96	2 trans	above lgr	no detect	0.666					431	718	2	5
4	94	3 trans	above lgr	no detect	0.877	0.520	0.481	0.513	0.481	2042	977	11	6
5	95	3 trans	above lgr	no detect	0.263					2419	717	8	9
6	96	3 trans	above lgr	no detect	0.608					472	718	2	5
7	94	4 trans	above lgr	no detect	0.390	0.394	0.319	0.337	0.305	4597	977	11	6
8	95	4 trans	above lgr	no detect	0.261					2439	717	8	9
9	96	4 trans	above lgr	no detect	0.602					477	718	2	5
10	94	2 trans	above lgr	no detect	1.071	0.693	0.692	0.679	0.667	1520	977	10	6
11	95	2 trans	above lgr	no detect, mcn	0.447					2227	1245	8	10
12	96	2 trans	above lgr	no detect, mcn	0.694					431	898	2	6
13	94	3 trans	above lgr	no detect	0.877	0.612	0.601	0.604	0.592	2042	977	11	6
14	95	3 trans	above lgr	no detect, mcn	0.412					2419	1245	8	10
15	96	3 trans	above lgr	no detect, mcn	0.633					472	898	2	6
16	94	4 trans	above lgr	no detect	0.390	0.464	0.399	0.396	0.375	4597	977	11	6
17	95	4 trans	above lgr	no detect, mcn	0.409					2439	1245	8	10
18	96	4 trans	above lgr	no detect, mcn	0.627					477	898	2	6
19	94	2 trans	above lgr	no detect	1.071	0.700	0.685	0.666	0.623	1520	977	10	6
20	95	2 trans	above lgr	no detect, mcn, lgr, lgr/mcn	0.438					2529	2340	9	19
21	96	2 trans	above lgr	no detect, mcn, lgr, lgr/mcn	0.729					517	1320	2	7
22	94	3 trans	above lgr	no detect	0.877	0.615	0.610	0.595	0.557	2042	977	11	6
23	95	3 trans	above lgr	no detect, mcn, lgr, lgr/mcn	0.423					3200	2340	11	19
24	96	3 trans	above lgr	no detect, mcn, lgr, lgr/mcn	0.626					603	1320	2	7
25	94	4 trans	above lgr	no detect	0.390	0.463	0.401	0.410	0.370	4597	977	11	6
26	95	4 trans	above lgr	no detect, mcn, lgr, lgr/mcn	0.412					3285	2340	11	19
27	96	4 trans	above lgr	no detect, mcn, lgr, lgr/mcn	0.616					612	1320	2	7
28	94	2 trans	above & @ lgr	no detect	1.071	0.647	0.830	0.648	0.664	1520	977	10	6
29	95	2 trans	above & @ lgr	no detect, mcn, lgr, lgr/mcn	0.643					28398	7441	108	44
30	96	2 trans	above & @ lgr	no detect, mcn, lgr, lgr/mcn	0.394					8682	3417	11	11
31	94	3 trans	above & @ lgr	no detect	0.877	0.597	0.746	0.638	0.649	2042	977	11	6
32	95	3 trans	above & @ lgr	no detect, mcn, lgr, lgr/mcn	0.635					30365	7441	114	44
33	96	3 trans	above & @ lgr	no detect, mcn, lgr, lgr/mcn	0.382					8953	3417	11	11
34	94	4 trans	above & @ lgr	no detect	0.390	0.455	0.496	0.599	0.600	4597	977	11	6
35	95	4 trans	above & @ lgr	no detect, mcn, lgr, lgr/mcn	0.632					30486	7441	114	44
36	96	4 trans	above & @ lgr	no detect, mcn, lgr, lgr/mcn	0.381					8967	3417	11	11

Wild fish, weekly-PI, per-project survival expansion, NMFS arrivals

Run	Year	Transpor Groups	In-river	D-value	94-96 Geom	94-95 Geom	94-96 Pooled	94-95 Pooled	BBsmolt Transpo	BBsmolt Inriver	Adults Transpo	Adults Inriver
1	94	2 trans	above lgr	no detect	1.635	0.718	0.748	0.732	0.752	1511	1482	10	6
2	95	2 trans	above lgr	no detect	0.343					2220	856	8	9
3	96	2 trans	above lgr	no detect	0.661					428	708	2	5
4	94	3 trans	above lgr	no detect	1.362	0.638	0.655	0.656	0.672	1994	1482	11	6
5	95	3 trans	above lgr	no detect	0.315					2414	856	8	9
6	96	3 trans	above lgr	no detect	0.604					469	708	2	5
7	94	4 trans	above lgr	no detect	0.621	0.488	0.441	0.439	0.435	4376	1482	11	6
8	95	4 trans	above lgr	no detect	0.313					2434	856	8	9
9	96	4 trans	above lgr	no detect	0.598					474	708	2	5
	94	2 trans	above lgr	no detect	1.635	0.846	0.929	0.841	0.889	1511	1482	10	6
10	95	2 trans	above lgr	no detect, mcn	0.528					2220	1467	8	10
11	96	2 trans	above lgr	no detect, mcn	0.700					428	898	2	6
	94	3 trans	above lgr	no detect	1.362	0.751	0.814	0.753	0.794	1994	1482	11	6
12	95	3 trans	above lgr	no detect, mcn	0.486					2414	1467	8	10
13	96	3 trans	above lgr	no detect, mcn	0.639					469	898	2	6
	94	4 trans	above lgr	no detect	0.621	0.574	0.547	0.504	0.514	4376	1482	11	6
14	95	4 trans	above lgr	no detect, mcn	0.482					2434	1467	8	10
15	96	4 trans	above lgr	no detect, mcn	0.632					474	898	2	6
	94	2 trans	above lgr	no detect	1.635	0.857	0.924	0.806	0.803	1511	1482	10	6
16	95	2 trans	above lgr	no detect, mcn, lgr, lgr/mcn	0.522					2518	2778	9	19
17	96	2 trans	above lgr	no detect, mcn, lgr, lgr/mcn	0.737					512	1320	2	7
	94	3 trans	above lgr	no detect	1.362	0.757	0.828	0.724	0.723	1994	1482	11	6
18	95	3 trans	above lgr	no detect, mcn, lgr, lgr/mcn	0.504					3193	2778	11	19
19	96	3 trans	above lgr	no detect, mcn, lgr, lgr/mcn	0.633					596	1320	2	7
	94	4 trans	above lgr	no detect	0.621	0.574	0.552	0.506	0.489	4376	1482	11	6
20	95	4 trans	above lgr	no detect, mcn, lgr, lgr/mcn	0.490					3282	2778	11	19
21	96	4 trans	above lgr	no detect, mcn, lgr, lgr/mcn	0.622					606	1320	2	7
	94	2 trans	above lgr	no detect	1.635	0.790	1.117	0.753	0.814	1511	1482	10	6
22	95	2 trans	above & @ lgr	no detect, mcn, lgr, lgr/mcn	0.763					28353	8813	108	44
23	96	2 trans	above & @ lgr	no detect, mcn, lgr, lgr/mcn	0.395					8667	3425	11	11
	94	3 trans	above lgr	no detect	1.362	0.733	1.013	0.741	0.796	1994	1482	11	6
24	95	3 trans	above & @ lgr	no detect, mcn, lgr, lgr/mcn	0.753					30330	8813	114	44
25	96	3 trans	above & @ lgr	no detect, mcn, lgr, lgr/mcn	0.383					8935	3425	11	11
	94	4 trans	above lgr	no detect	0.621	0.563	0.682	0.699	0.739	4376	1482	11	6
26	95	4 trans	above & @ lgr	no detect, mcn, lgr, lgr/mcn	0.750					30457	8813	114	44
27	96	4 trans	above & @ lgr	no detect, mcn, lgr, lgr/mcn	0.383					8950	3425	11	11

Wild fish, weekly-PI, per-mile survival expansion, NMFS arrivals

Run	Year	Transport	Groups	In-river	D-value	94-96 Geom	94-95 Geom	94-96 Pooled	94-95 Pooled	BBsmolt Transpo	BBsmolt Inriver	Adults Transpo	Adults Inriver
1	94	2 trans	above lgr	no detect	1.272	0.605	0.624	0.608	0.617	1511	1153	10	6
2	95	2 trans	above lgr	no detect	0.306					2220	766	8	9
3	96	2 trans	above lgr	no detect	0.569					428	609	2	5
4	94	3 trans	above lgr	no detect	1.060	0.538	0.547	0.544	0.551	1994	1153	11	6
5	95	3 trans	above lgr	no detect	0.282					2414	766	8	9
6	96	3 trans	above lgr	no detect	0.520					469	609	2	5
7	94	4 trans	above lgr	no detect	0.475	0.409	0.364	0.361	0.353	4453	1153	11	6
8	95	4 trans	above lgr	no detect	0.280					2434	766	8	9
9	96	4 trans	above lgr	no detect	0.514					474	609	2	5
10	94	2 trans	above lgr	no detect	1.272	0.713	0.775	0.708	0.743	1511	1153	10	6
11	95	2 trans	above lgr	no detect, mcn	0.473					2220	1312	8	10
	96	2 trans	above lgr	no detect, mcn	0.602					428	773	2	6
12	94	3 trans	above lgr	no detect	1.060	0.633	0.679	0.634	0.664	1994	1153	11	6
13	95	3 trans	above lgr	no detect, mcn	0.435					2414	1312	8	10
	96	3 trans	above lgr	no detect, mcn	0.550					469	773	2	6
14	94	4 trans	above lgr	no detect	0.475	0.481	0.452	0.420	0.425	4453	1153	11	6
15	95	4 trans	above lgr	no detect, mcn	0.431					2434	1312	8	10
	96	4 trans	above lgr	no detect, mcn	0.544					474	773	2	6
16	94	2 trans	above lgr	no detect, mcn, lgr, lgr/mcn	1.272	0.722	0.771	0.690	0.686	1511	1153	10	6
17	95	2 trans	above lgr	no detect, mcn, lgr, lgr/mcn	0.467					2518	2484	9	19
	96	2 trans	above lgr	no detect, mcn, lgr, lgr/mcn	0.634					512	1136	2	7
18	94	3 trans	above lgr	no detect, mcn, lgr, lgr/mcn	1.060	0.638	0.691	0.619	0.617	1994	1153	11	6
19	95	3 trans	above lgr	no detect, mcn, lgr, lgr/mcn	0.451					3193	2484	11	19
	96	3 trans	above lgr	no detect, mcn, lgr, lgr/mcn	0.544					596	1136	2	7
20	94	4 trans	above lgr	no detect, mcn, lgr, lgr/mcn	0.475	0.481	0.456	0.429	0.414	4453	1153	11	6
21	95	4 trans	above lgr	no detect, mcn, lgr, lgr/mcn	0.438					3282	2484	11	19
	96	4 trans	above lgr	no detect, mcn, lgr, lgr/mcn	0.535					606	1136	2	7
22	94	2 trans	above lgr	no detect	1.272	0.666	0.932	0.658	0.714	1511	1153	10	6
23	95	2 trans	above & @ lgr	no detect, mcn, lgr, lgr/mcn	0.682					28353	7883	108	44
	96	2 trans	above & @ lgr	no detect, mcn, lgr, lgr/mcn	0.340					8667	2947	11	11
24	94	3 trans	above lgr	no detect	1.060	0.618	0.845	0.648	0.699	1994	1153	11	6
25	95	3 trans	above & @ lgr	no detect, mcn, lgr, lgr/mcn	0.673					30330	7883	114	44
	96	3 trans	above & @ lgr	no detect, mcn, lgr, lgr/mcn	0.330					8935	2947	11	11
26	94	4 trans	above lgr	no detect	0.475	0.472	0.564	0.609	0.647	4453	1153	11	6
27	95	4 trans	above & @ lgr	no detect, mcn, lgr, lgr/mcn	0.671					30457	7883	114	44
	96	4 trans	above & @ lgr	no detect, mcn, lgr-, lgr/mcn	0.329					8950	2947	11	11

5 CRiSPT5 (same as CRiSP T4)

Run	Year	Transport	Groups	In-river	D-value	94-96 Geom	94-95 Geom	94-96 Pooled	94-95 Pooled	BBsmolt Transpo	BBsmolts Inriver	Adults Transpo	Adults Inriver
1	94	2 trans	above lgr	no detect	1.167	0.450	0.514	0.480	0.522	1512	1059	10	6
2	95	2 trans	above lgr	no detect	0.227					2226	568	8	9
3	96	2 trans	above lgr	no detect	0.343					444	381	2	5
4	94	3 trans	above lgr	no detect	0.958	0.395	0.446	0.426	0.463	2026	1059	11	6
5	95	3 trans	above lgr	no detect	0.208					2427	568	8	9
6	96	3 trans	above lgr	no detect	0.309					493	381	2	5
7	94	4 trans	above lgr	no detect	0.412	0.296	0.291	0.275	0.288	4711	1059	11	6
8	95	4 trans	above lgr	no detect	0.206					2450	568	8	9
9	96	4 trans	above lgr	no detect	0.306					498	381	2	5
	94	2 trans	above lgr	no detect	1.167	0.582	0.688	0.596	0.658	1512	1059	10	6
10	95	2 trans	above lgr	no detect, mcn	0.406					2226	1130	8	10
11	96	2 trans	above lgr	no detect, mcn	0.416					444	554	2	6
	94	3 trans	above lgr	no detect	0.958	0.511	0.597	0.529	0.584	2026	1059	11	6
12	95	3 trans	above lgr	no detect, mcn	0.372					2427	1130	8	10
13	96	3 trans	above lgr	no detect, mcn	0.375					493	554	2	6
	94	4 trans	above lgr	no detect	0.412	0.383	0.390	0.342	0.363	4711	1059	11	6
14	95	4 trans	above lgr	no detect, mcn	0.369					2450	1130	8	10
15	96	4 trans	above lgr	no detect, mcn	0.370					498	554	2	6
	94	2 trans	above lgr	no detect	1.167	0.552	0.615	0.520	0.525	1512	1059	10	6
16	95	2 trans	above lgr	no detect, mcn, lgr, lgr/mcn	0.324					2528	1732	9	19
17	96	2 trans	above lgr	no detect, mcn, lgr, lgr/mcn	0.445					537	838	2	7
	94	3 trans	above lgr	no detect	0.958	0.481	0.545	0.462	0.467	2026	1059	11	6
18	95	3 trans	above lgr	no detect, mcn, lgr, lgr/mcn	0.310					3229	1732	11	19
19	96	3 trans	above lgr	no detect, mcn, lgr, lgr/mcn	0.374					639	838	2	7
	94	4 trans	above lgr	no detect	0.412	0.357	0.352	0.313	0.305	4711	1059	11	6
20	95	4 trans	above lgr	no detect, mcn, lgr, lgr/mcn	0.301					3329	1732	11	19
21	96	4 trans	above lgr	no detect, mcn, lgr, lgr/mcn	0.368					650	838	2	7
	94	2 trans	above lgr	no detect	1.167	0.504	0.711	0.453	0.479	1512	1059	10	6
22	95	2 trans	above & @ lgr	no detect, mcn, lgr, lgr/mcn	0.434					28394	5015	108	44
23	96	2 trans	above & @ lgr	no detect, mcn, lgr, lgr/mcn	0.253					8736	2211	11	11
	94	3 trans	above lgr	no detect	0.958	0.464	0.639	0.445	0.468	2026	1059	11	6
24	95	3 trans	above & @ lgr	no detect, mcn, lgr, lgr/mcn	0.427					30449	5015	114	44
25	96	3 trans	above & @ lgr	no detect, mcn, lgr, lgr/mcn	0.244					9059	2211	11	11
	94	4 trans	above lgr	no detect	0.412	0.349	0.418	0.416	0.430	4711	1059	11	6
26	95	4 trans	above & @ lgr	no detect, mcn, lgr, lgr/mcn	0.425					30591	5015	114	44
27	96	4 trans	above & @ lgr	no detect, mcn, lgr, lgr/mcn	0.244					9076	2211	11	11

6: CRiSPT4

Run	Year	Transpor	Groups	In-river	D-value	94-96 Geom	94-95 Geom	94-96 Pooled	94-95 Pooled	BBsmolt Transpo Inriver	BBsmolt Inriver	Adults Transpo Inriver	Adults Inriver
1	94	2 trans	above lgr	no detect	1.167	0.450	0.514	0.480	0.522	1512	1059	10	6
2	95	2 trans	above lgr	no detect	0.227					2226	568	8	9
3	96	2 trans	above lgr	no detect	0.343					444	381	2	5
4	94	3 trans	above lgr	no detect	0.958	0.395	0.446	0.426	0.463	2026	1059	11	6
5	95	3 trans	above lgr	no detect	0.208					2427	568	8	9
6	96	3 trans	above lgr	no detect	0.309					493	381	2	5
7	94	4 trans	above lgr	no detect	0.412	0.296	0.291	0.275	0.288	4711	1059	11	6
8	95	4 trans	above lgr	no detect	0.206					2450	568	8	9
9	96	4 trans	above lgr	no detect	0.306					498	381	2	5
10	94	2 trans	above lgr	no detect	1.167	0.582	0.688	0.596	0.658	1512	1059	10	6
11	95	2 trans	above lgr	no detect, mcn	0.406					2226	1130	8	10
12	96	2 trans	above lgr	no detect, mcn	0.416					444	554	2	6
13	94	3 trans	above lgr	no detect	0.958	0.511	0.597	0.529	0.584	2026	1059	11	6
14	95	3 trans	above lgr	no detect, mcn	0.372					2427	1130	8	10
15	96	3 trans	above lgr	no detect, mcn	0.375					493	554	2	6
16	94	4 trans	above lgr	no detect	0.412	0.383	0.390	0.342	0.363	4711	1059	11	6
17	95	4 trans	above lgr	no detect, mcn	0.369					2450	1130	8	10
18	96	4 trans	above lgr	no detect, mcn	0.370					498	554	2	6
19	94	2 trans	above lgr	no detect	1.167	0.552	0.615	0.520	0.525	1512	1059	10	6
20	95	2 trans	above lgr	no detect, mcn, lgr, lgr/mcn	0.324					2528	1732	9	19
21	96	2 trans	above lgr	no detect, mcn, lgr, lgr/mcn	0.445					537	838	2	7
22	94	3 trans	above lgr	no detect	0.958	0.481	0.545	0.462	0.467	2026	1059	11	6
23	95	3 trans	above lgr	no detect, mcn, lgr, lgr/mcn	0.310					3229	1732	11	19
24	96	3 trans	above lgr	no detect, mcn, lgr, lgr/mcn	0.374					639	838	2	7
25	94	4 trans	above lgr	no detect	0.412	0.357	0.352	0.313	0.305	4711	1059	11	6
26	95	4 trans	above lgr	no detect, mcn, lgr, lgr/mcn	0.301					3329	1732	11	19
27	96	4 trans	above lgr	no detect, mcn, lgr, lgr/mcn	0.368					650	838	2	7
28	94	2 trans	above & @ lgr	no detect	1.167	0.504	0.711	0.453	0.479	1512	1059	10	6
29	95	2 trans	above & @ lgr	no detect, mcn, lgr, gr/mcn	0.434					28394	5015	108	44
30	96	2 trans	above & @ lgr	no detect, mcn, lgr, gr/mcn	0.253					8736	2211	11	11
31	94	3 trans	above & @ lgr	no detect	0.958	0.464	0.639	0.445	0.468	2026	1059	11	6
32	95	3 trans	above & @ lgr	no detect, mcn, lgr, lgr/mcn	0.427					30449	5015	114	44
33	96	3 trans	above & @ lgr	no detect, mcn, lgr, lgr/mcn	0.244					9059	2211	11	11
34	94	4 trans	above & @ lgr	no detect	0.412	0.349	0.418	0.416	0.430	4711	1059	11	6
35	95	4 trans	above & @ lgr	no detect, mcn, lgr, lgr/mcn	0.425					30591	5015	114	44
36	96	4 trans	above & @ lgr	no detect, mcn, lgr, lgr/mcn	0.244					9076	2211	11	11

FLUSHT5

Run	Year	Transpor	Groups	In-river	D-value	94-96 Geom	94-95 Geom	94-96 Pooled	94-95 Pooled	BBsmolt Transpo	BBsmolt Inriver	Adults Transpo	Adults Inriver
1	94	2 trans	above lgr	no detect	0.240	0.216	0.139	0.236	0.134	1503	216	10	6
2	95	2 trans	above lgr	no detect	0.080					2219	200	8	9
3	96	2 trans	above lgr	no detect	0.523					430	563	2	5
4	94	3 trans	above lgr	no detect	0.195	0.190	0.120	0.209	0.118	2039	216	11	6
5	95	3 trans	above lgr	no detect	0.074					2422	200	8	9
6	96	3 trans	above lgr	no detect	0.477					473	563	2	5
7	94	4 trans	above lgr	no detect	0.066	0.131	0.069	0.115	0.062	6031	216	11	6
8	95	4 trans	above lgr	no detect	0.073					2451	200	8	9
9	96	4 trans	above lgr	no detect	0.472					478	563	2	5
10	94	2 trans	above lgr	no detect	0.240	0.299	0.218	0.327	0.231	1503	216	10	6
11	95	2 trans	above lgr	no detect, mcn	0.198					2219	549	8	10
12	96	2 trans	above lgr	no detect, mcn	0.562					430	726	2	6
13	94	3 trans	above lgr	no detect	0.195	0.262	0.188	0.289	0.204	2039	216	11	6
14	95	3 trans	above lgr	no detect, mcn	0.181					2422	549	8	10
15	96	3 trans	above lgr	no detect, mcn	0.512					473	726	2	6
16	94	4 trans	above lgr	no detect	0.066	0.181	0.109	0.159	0.107	6031	216	11	6
17	95	4 trans	above lgr	no detect, mcn	0.179					2451	549	8	10
18	96	4 trans	above lgr	no detect, mcn	0.507					478	726	2	6
19	94	2 trans	above lgr	no detect	0.240	0.302	0.216	0.335	0.235	1503	216	10	6
20	95	2 trans	above lgr	no detect, mcn, lgr, lgr/mcn	0.194					2516	1029	9	19
21	96	2 trans	above lgr	no detect, mcn, lgr, lgr/mcn	0.592					515	1067	2	7
22	94	3 trans	above lgr	no detect	0.195	0.263	0.190	0.296	0.208	2039	216	11	6
23	95	3 trans	above lgr	no detect, mcn, lgr, lgr/mcn	0.185					3223	1029	11	19
24	96	3 trans	above lgr	no detect, mcn, lgr, lgr/mcn	0.505					603	1067	2	7
25	94	4 trans	above lgr	no detect	0.066	0.180	0.108	0.173	0.117	6031	216	11	6
26	95	4 trans	above lgr	no detect, mcn, lgr, lgr/mcn	0.178					3353	1029	11	19
27	96	4 trans	above lgr	no detect, mcn, lgr, lgr/mcn	0.497					613	1067	2	7
28	94	2 trans	above lgr	no detect	0.240	0.279	0.261	0.344	0.277	1503	216	10	6
29	95	2 trans	above & @ lgr	no detect, mcn, lgr, lgr/mcn	0.285					28343	3285	108	44
30	96	2 trans	above & @ lgr	no detect, mcn, lgr, lgr/mcn	0.318					8677	2760	11	11
31	94	3 trans	above lgr	no detect	0.195	0.256	0.233	0.337	0.270	2039	216	11	6
32	95	3 trans	above & @ lgr	no detect, mcn, lgr, lgr/mcn	0.280					30417	3285	114	44
33	96	3 trans	above & @ lgr	no detect, mcn, lgr, lgr/mcn	0.308					8956	2760	11	11
34	94	4 trans	above lgr	no detect	0.066	0.178	0.135	0.306	0.239	6031	216	11	6
35	95	4 trans	above & @ lgr	no detect, mcn, lgr, lgr/mcn	0.278					30602	3285	114	44
36	96	4 trans	above & @ lgr	no detect, mcn, lgr, lgr/mcn	0.308					8971	2760	11	11

FLUSHT4

Run	Year	Transpor	Groups	In-river	D-value	94-96 Geom	94-95 Geom	94-96 Pooled	94-95 Pooled	BBsmolt Transpo	BBsmolt Inriver	Adults Transpo	Adults Inriver
1	94	2 trans	above lgr	no detect	0.477	0.207	0.139	0.248	0.172	1537	440	10	6
2	95	2 trans	above lgr	no detect	0.040					2249	102	8	9
3	96	2 trans	above lgr	no detect	0.463					439	507	2	5
4	94	3 trans	above lgr	no detect	0.382	0.180	0.118	0.217	0.150	2109	440	11	6
5	95	3 trans	above lgr	no detect	0.037					2473	102	8	9
6	96	3 trans	above lgr	no detect	0.418					486	507	2	5
7	94	4 trans	above lgr	no detect	0.144	0.129	0.072	0.128	0.085	5615	440	11	6
8	95	4 trans	above lgr	no detect	0.036					2502	102	8	9
9	96	4 trans	above lgr	no detect	0.413					491	507	2	5
	94	2 trans	above lgr	no detect	0.477	0.376	0.316	0.372	0.306	1537	440	10	6
10	95	2 trans	above lgr	no detect, mcn	0.210					2249	589	8	10
11	96	2 trans	above lgr	no detect, mcn	0.533					439	702	2	6
	94	3 trans	above lgr	no detect	0.382	0.327	0.270	0.326	0.267	2109	440	11	6
12	95	3 trans	above lgr	no detect, mcn	0.191					2473	589	8	10
13	96	3 trans	above lgr	no detect, mcn	0.482					486	702	2	6
	94	4 trans	above lgr	no detect	0.144	0.234	0.164	0.192	0.151	5615	440	11	6
14	95	4 trans	above lgr	no detect, mcn	0.188					2502	589	8	10
15	96	4 trans	above lgr	no detect, mcn	0.477					491	702	2	6
	94	2 trans	above lgr	no detect	0.477	0.378	0.312	0.365	0.286	1537	440	10	6
16	95	2 trans	above lgr	no detect, mcn, lgr, lgr/mcn	0.204					2567	1103	9	19
17	96	2 trans	above lgr	no detect, mcn, lgr, lgr/mcn	0.557					529	1031	2	7
	94	3 trans	above lgr	no detect	0.382	0.325	0.270	0.318	0.249	2109	440	11	6
18	95	3 trans	above lgr	no detect, mcn, lgr, lgr/mcn	0.191					3345	1103	11	19
19	96	3 trans	above lgr	no detect, mcn, lgr, lgr/mcn	0.470					627	1031	2	7
	94	4 trans	above lgr	no detect	0.144	0.230	0.162	0.198	0.149	5615	440	11	6
20	95	4 trans	above lgr	no detect, mcn, lgr, lgr/mcn	0.184					3475	1103	11	19
21	96	4 trans	above lgr	no detect, mcn, lgr, lgr/mcn	0.462					637	1031	2	7
	94	2 trans	above lgr	no detect	0.477	0.360	0.394	0.373	0.331	1537	440	10	6
22	95	2 trans	above & @ lgr	no detect, mcn, lgr, lgr/mcn	0.325					28552	3781	108	44
23	96	2 trans	above & @ lgr	no detect, mcn, lgr, lgr/mcn	0.301					8714	2623	11	11
	94	3 trans	above lgr	no detect	0.382	0.328	0.349	0.364	0.320	2109	440	11	6
24	95	3 trans	above & @ lgr	no detect, mcn, lgr, lgr/mcn	0.318					30833	3781	114	44
25	96	3 trans	above & @ lgr	no detect, mcn, lgr, lgr/mcn	0.291					9023	2623	11	11
	94	4 trans	above lgr	no detect	0.144	0.236	0.213	0.334	0.288	5615	440	11	6
26	95	4 trans	above & @ lgr	no detect, mcn, lgr, lgr/mcn	0.316					31018	3781	114	44
27	96	4 trans	above & @ lgr	no detect, mcn, lgr, lgr/mcn	0.290					9040	2623	11	11

All fish, daily, per-project survival expansion, IDFG arrivals

Run	Year	Transpor	Groups	In-river	D-value	94-96 Geom	94-95 Geom	94-96 Pooled	94-95 Pooled	BBsmolt Transpo	BBsmolt Inriver	Adults Transpo	Adults Inriver
1	94	2 trans	above lgr	no detect	0.990	0.819	0.726	0.804	0.716	1520	903	10	6
2	95	2 trans	above lgr	no detect	0.532					2227	1334	8	9
3	96	2 trans	above lgr	no detect	1.041					431	1123	2	5
4	94	3 trans	above lgr	no detect	0.811	0.723	0.630	0.715	0.635	2042	903	11	6
5	95	3 trans	above lgr	no detect	0.490					2419	1334	8	9
6	96	3 trans	above lgr	no detect	0.951					472	1123	2	5
7	94	4 trans	above lgr	no detect	0.370	0.553	0.424	0.477	0.410	4479	903	11	6
8	95	4 trans	above lgr	no detect	0.486					2439	1334	8	9
9	96	4 trans	above lgr	no detect	0.942					477	1123	2	5
10	94	2 trans	above lgr	no detect	0.990	0.883	0.826	0.898	0.847	1520	903	10	6
11	95	2 trans	above lgr	no detect, mcn	0.689					2227	1918	8	10
	96	2 trans	above lgr	no detect, mcn	1.009					431	1306	2	6
12	94	3 trans	above lgr	no detect	0.811	0.779	0.717	0.798	0.751	2042	903	11	6
13	95	3 trans	above lgr	no detect, mcn	0.634					2419	1918	8	10
	96	3 trans	above lgr	no detect, mcn	0.921					472	1306	2	6
14	94	4 trans	above lgr	no detect	0.370	0.596	0.482	0.533	0.484	4479	903	11	6
15	95	4 trans	above lgr	no detect, mcn	0.629					2439	1918	8	10
	96	4 trans	above lgr	no detect, mcn	0.913					477	1306	2	6
16	94	2 trans	above lgr	no detect	0.990	0.838	0.775	0.850	0.778	1520	903	10	6
17	95	2 trans	above lgr	no detect, mcn, lgr, lgr/mcn	0.607					2529	3240	9	19
	96	2 trans	above lgr	no detect, mcn, lgr, lgr/mcn	0.980					517	1774	2	7
18	94	3 trans	above lgr	no detect	0.811	0.737	0.689	0.759	0.696	2042	903	11	6
19	95	3 trans	above lgr	no detect, mcn, lgr, lgr/mcn	0.586					3200	3240	11	19
	96	3 trans	above lgr	no detect, mcn, lgr, lgr/mcn	0.841					603	1774	2	7
20	94	4 trans	above lgr	no detect	0.370	0.559	0.459	0.530	0.470	4479	903	11	6
21	95	4 trans	above lgr	no detect, mcn, lgr, lgr/mcn	0.571					3285	3240	11	19
	96	4 trans	above lgr	no detect, mcn, lgr, lgr/mcn	0.828					612	1774	2	7
22	94	2 trans	above lgr	no detect	0.990	0.725	0.898	0.791	0.815	1520	903	10	6
23	95	2 trans	above & @ lgr	no detect, mcn, lgr, lgr/mcn	0.816					28398	9435	108	44
	96	2 trans	above & @ lgr	no detect, mcn, lgr, lgr/mcn	0.472					8682	4100	11	11
24	94	3 trans	above lgr	no detect	0.811	0.669	0.808	0.778	0.798	2042	903	11	6
25	95	3 trans	above & @ lgr	no detect, mcn, lgr, lgr/mcn	0.805					30365	9435	114	44
	96	3 trans	above & @ lgr	no detect, mcn, lgr, lgr/mcn	0.458					8953	4100	11	11
26	94	4 trans	above lgr	no detect	0.370	0.514	0.544	0.733	0.739	4479	903	11	6
27	95	4 trans	above & @ lgr	no detect, mcn, lgr, lgr/mcn	0.802					30486	9435	114	44
	96	4 trans	above & @ lgr	no detect, mcn, lgr, lgr/mcn	0.457					8967	4100	11	11

Wild fish, weekly-PI, per-mile survival expansion, IDFG arrivals

Run	Year	Transpor Groups	In-river	D-value	94-96 Geom	94-95 Geom	94-96 Pooled	94-95 Pooled	BBsmolt Transpo	BBsmolt Inriver	Adults Transpo	Adults Inriver
1	94	2 trans above lgr	no detect	0.943	0.686	0.642	0.670	0.626	1511	855	10	6
2	95	2 trans above lgr	no detect	0.437					2220	1093	8	9
3	96	2 trans above lgr	no detect	0.782					428	837	2	5
4	94	3 trans above lgr	no detect	0.786	0.609	0.562	0.600	0.560	1994	855	11	6
5	95	3 trans above lgr	no detect	0.402					2414	1093	8	9
6	96	3 trans above lgr	no detect	0.715					469	837	2	5
7	94	4 trans above lgr	no detect	0.352	0.463	0.375	0.397	0.358	4453	855	11	6
8	95	4 trans above lgr	no detect	0.399					2434	1093	8	9
9	96	4 trans above lgr	no detect	0.707					474	837	2	5
10	94	2 trans above lgr	no detect, mcn	0.943	0.757	0.746	0.764	0.752	1511	855	10	6
11	95	2 trans above lgr	no detect, mcn	0.590					2220	1639	8	10
12	96	2 trans above lgr	no detect, mcn	0.780					428	1001	2	6
13	94	3 trans above lgr	no detect, mcn	0.786	0.609	0.653	0.613	0.672	1994	855	11	6
14	95	3 trans above lgr	no detect, mcn	0.543					2414	1639	8	10
15	96	3 trans above lgr	no detect, mcn	0.529					2518	2811	9	19
16	94	4 trans above lgr	no detect, mcn	0.352	0.515	0.518	0.462	0.447	4453	855	11	6
17	95	4 trans above lgr	no detect, mcn	0.762					512	1364	2	7
18	96	4 trans above lgr	no detect, mcn	0.510					3193	2811	11	19
19	94	2 trans above lgr	no detect, mcn, lgr, lgr/mcn	0.943	0.674	0.785	0.671	0.972	1511	855	10	6
20	95	2 trans above lgr	no detect, mcn, lgr, lgr/mcn	0.654					596	1364	2	7
21	96	2 trans above lgr	no detect, mcn, lgr, lgr/mcn	0.496					3282	2811	11	19
22	94	3 trans above lgr	no detect, mcn, lgr, lgr/mcn	0.786	0.711	0.711	0.715	0.853	1994	855	11	6
23	95	3 trans above lgr	no detect, mcn, lgr, lgr/mcn	0.643					606	1364	2	7
24	96	3 trans above lgr	no detect, mcn, lgr, lgr/mcn	0.711					28353	8210	108	44
25	94	4 trans above lgr	no detect, mcn, lgr, lgr/mcn	0.352	0.449	0.359	0.628	0.398	4453	855	11	6
26	95	4 trans above lgr	no detect, mcn, lgr, lgr/mcn	0.366					8667	3176	11	11
27	96	4 trans above lgr	no detect, mcn, lgr, lgr/mcn	0.701					30330	8210	114	44
28	94	2 trans above & @ lgr	no detect, mcn, lgr, lgr/mcn	0.943	0.616	0.579	0.662	0.477	1511	855	10	6
29	95	2 trans above & @ lgr	no detect, mcn, lgr, lgr/mcn	0.355					8935	3176	11	11
30	96	2 trans above & @ lgr	no detect, mcn, lgr, lgr/mcn	0.698					30457	8210	114	44
31	94	3 trans above & @ lgr	no detect, mcn, lgr, lgr/mcn	0.786	0.475	0.528	0.442	0.477	1994	855	11	6
32	95	3 trans above & @ lgr	no detect, mcn, lgr, lgr/mcn	0.355					8950	3176	11	11
33	96	3 trans above & @ lgr	no detect, mcn, lgr, lgr/mcn	0.385					8259	8210	11	11
34	94	4 trans above & @ lgr	no detect, mcn, lgr, lgr/mcn	0.352	0.458	0.500	0.627	0.654	4453	855	11	6
35	95	4 trans above & @ lgr	no detect, mcn, lgr, lgr/mcn	0.710					26019	8210	99	44
36	96	4 trans above & @ lgr	no detect, mcn, lgr, lgr/mcn	0.384					8264	3176	11	11